BASICS

INTERIOR ARC

02

Graeme Brooker
Sally Stone

CW00505184

ava | Academia
the environment of learning

An AVA Book

Published by AVA Publishing SA
Rue des Fontenailles 16
Case Postale
1000 Lausanne 6
Switzerland

Tel: +41 786 005 109
Email: enquiries@avabooks.ch

Distributed by Thames & Hudson (ex-North America)
181a High Holborn
London WC1V 7QX
United Kingdom

Tel: +44 20 7845 5000
Fax: +44 20 7845 5055
Email: sales@thameshudson.co.uk
www.thamesandhudson.com

Distributed in the USA & Canada by:
Watson-Guptill Publications
770 Broadway
New York, New York 10003
USA

Fax: +1 646 654 5487
Email: info@watsonguptill.com
www.watsonguptill.com

English Language Support Office
AVA Publishing (UK) Ltd.

Tel: +44 1903 204 455
Email: enquiries@avabooks.co.uk

Copyright © AVA Publishing SA 2008

The authors assert their moral right to the work.

All rights reserved. No part of this publication may
be reproduced, stored in a retrieval system or
transmitted in any form or by any means, electronic,
mechanical, photocopying, recording or otherwise,
without permission of the copyright holder.

ISBN 2-940373-71-X and 978-2-940373-71-0

10 9 8 7 6 5 4 3 2 1

Design by John F McGill

Production by
AVA Book Production Pte. Ltd., Singapore

Tel: +65 6334 8173
Fax: +65 6259 9830
Email: production@avabooks.com.sg

All reasonable attempts have been made to
trace, clear and credit the copyright holders
of the images reproduced in this book. However,
if any credits have been inadvertently omitted,
the publisher will endeavour to incorporate
amendments in future editions.

Name:
The Haçienda (see pp 050+051)

Location:
Manchester, England

Date:
1982

Designer:
Ben Kelly Design

Contents

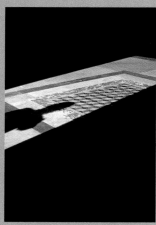
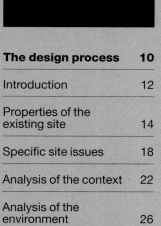

Context + Environment

Contents

Introduction

The aim of this book is to provide an informative and readable investigation into the practice of designing interior space. The focus of this investigation will be on the analysis and understanding of the elements based both inside and outside of the existing building that influence and affect the interior space.

The setting in which an interior is situated provides its context. The analysis of context is the understanding of the *genius loci*, or the spirit of the place and its physical, visual, aural and prevailing character. The environment has much more to do with the natural and climatic conditions of the area. It is the study of the weather, the atmosphere, the ambience of the place. The two are examined as distinct but concurring, inextricably linked entities. They are not mutually exclusive and there are inevitable overlaps both in the influence they have on the design and in the way in which they are examined.

The particular characteristics of a specific situation can influence the redesign of an existing space, and the manner in which these defining qualities can be examined and exploited will be explored through the analysis of case studies and running commentary.

The book will propose a method of interpretation, evaluation and utilisation of contextual issues of the urban form and the physical factors dictated by the natural world around us. It will examine the influence of these on the design of the interior and the remodelling of the existing building.

By uncovering the links between an interior and its context and environment, the designer can employ effective sustainable and energy-efficient strategies, which are becoming of ever-increasing importance to all designers. This book also aims to show the various strategies available to the designer working with interiors both new and old. These cover both the manner of the design and the ways in which the spaces are intended to be used.

An approach to the design of interiors based on the perceptive and discriminating reading of the existing or proposed building, combined with a sympathetic attitude towards sustainable and low-energy strategies can produce both eloquent and appropriate results.

Name:
Sackler Galleries, Royal Academy of Arts (see pp 166+167)
Location:
London, England
Date:
1991
Designer:
Foster + Partners

Context + Environment

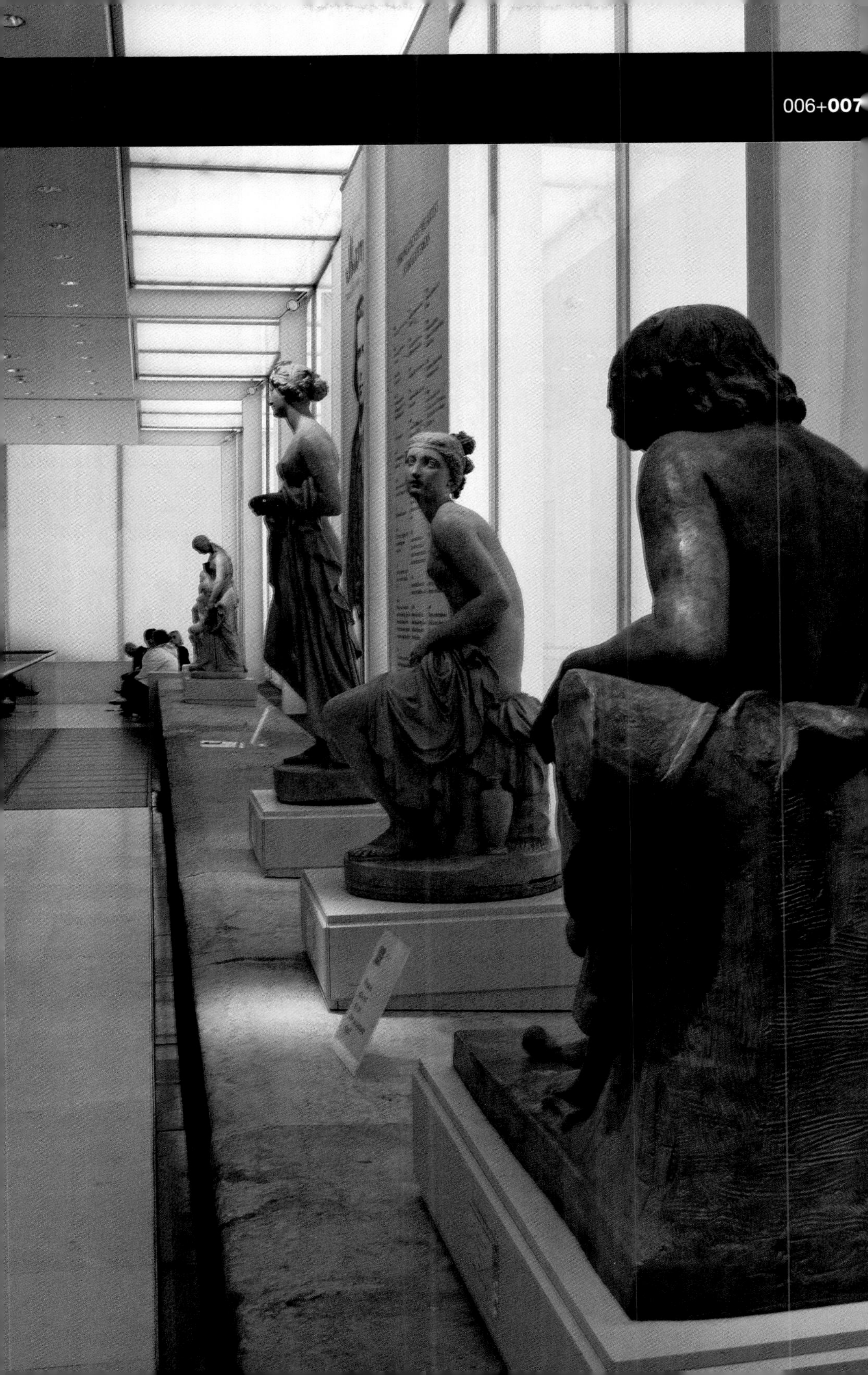

How to get the most out of this book

This book introduces different aspects of the role that contextual and environmental factors can play in the redesign of an interior, via dedicated chapters for each topic. Each chapter provides clear examples from leading architecture and design practices, annotated to explain the reasons behind the design choices made.

Section headers
Each chapter is broken down into sub-sections, the title of which can be found at the top left-hand corner of each spread.

Section introduction
Each sub-section is introduced by a short paragraph, outlining the content to be covered.

Page numbers
Page numbers are displayed in the top right-hand corner of each spread.

The Brundtland Commission (convened by the United Nations in 1983) published its final report in 1987, *Our Common Future*. This defines sustainable development as 'development that meets the needs of the present without compromising the ability of future generations to meet their own needs.' This definition is deliberately imprecise and allows for many different readings and interpretations, while still providing a goal or standard to aspire to.

Facing page:
Section
The protective overlapping floors are clearly visible.

Right:
The building at night
The computer-generated, organic shape of the building is a dramatic element on the skyline.

Environmental awareness: Focus study 1

Name:
City Hall

Location:
London, England

Date:
2002

Designer:
Foster + Partners

New techniques and technology are constantly helping designers to predict environmental conditions, facilitating more sustainable, environmentally sensitive and efficient designs.

Foster + Partners as a practice are very conscious of sustainable design and have acquired a reputation for creating buildings that are sensitive to environmental concerns. To this end they have developed their own variation on the accepted definition of sustainable design. The practice describes it as the process of creating buildings that are energy efficient, healthy, comfortable, flexible in use and designed for a long life.

The City Hall, or Greater London Authority Building, is located in a pivotal position opposite the tourist attractions of the Tower of London and London Bridge on the South Bank of the river Thames. The building is basically very simple; a series of stacked floor slabs enclosed by a steel and glass skin. But its unique shape is derived from sophisticated computer modelling software that has formalised the movement and impact of direct sunlight on the building. The computer calculated how the sun would strike the building on every day of the year and then adapted the design accordingly. Millions of calculations have then determined the shape and opacity of each piece of glass slotted into the skin of the building.

The south-facing side receives the most sunlight. The slipped stack of slab floors alleviates the problems associated with solar gain. Each overhangs the one below it and therefore provides a degree of shading.

The north-facing façade, which looks on to the Thames, receives minimal direct sunlight and therefore the glazing is unshaded. All the façades also have mechanically operated blinds to maximise shading.

Foster + Partners designed the building to minimise energy use and consume 75 per cent less energy than a traditional air conditioned office building. The building utilises natural ventilation systems and environmental control systems that incorporate naturally chilled groundwater drawn from boreholes that were sunk hundreds of feet below the building into the London Clay. The building contains a full-height 730-metre-long ramp that ascends the ten storeys and arrives at a rooftop viewing platform. Like the Reichstag in Berlin, which Foster also designed, the ramp not only gives dramatic views across the city but it also enables visitors to look down into the debating chamber and on to the politicians below.

Our Common Future
The Brundtland Commission's final report was drawn up by an international group of politicians in consultation with experts on environmental development. It is thought of as a seminal document because it brought to the attention of the world the need to consider sustainable design and created the context for environmental conservation.

Above:
Debating hall
The spiralling ramp offers a vast and dramatic panorama of the city and an intense, focussed view of the debating chamber.

Chapter footers
The current chapter title is displayed in the bottom left-hand corner of each spread.

Boxed texts
Additional points of interest to the reader are displayed in grey boxes.

Section footers
Past, present and future sub-sections are listed in the bottom right-hand corner of each spread. The current sub-section is highlighted in bold.

The examples shown include a mix of photographs, sketches and drawings, which, when combined with detailed analysis in the text, create a unique and fascinating insight into the world of interior architecture and design.

Pull quotes
Additional quotes from subject experts and practitioners.

Location

040+**041**

'The building that is to be remodelled is also part of its own context. The quality of the individual spaces, the relationship of one room with another and of each floor with the one below or above, the positions of the doors, the windows and the circulation areas all contribute to the intricate composition of the existing building.'

Graeme Brooker and Sally Stone

Location: Focus study 2

Name:
Architectural
Documentation Centre

Location:
Madrid, Spain

Date:
2004

Designer:
Aparicio + Fernández-Elorza

Sites that have unusual or extraordinary characteristics can lead the designer to create an equally remarkable interior. Within this project, the quite extreme qualities of the site and its existing structures have led to a daring and innovative intervention by the architects in order to realise the necessary requirements of the project.

The Architectural Documentation Centre was formed within the long arcade of a disused building and the underground platform below it, in the Nuevos Ministerios district. Two main principles guided the design: firstly, the existing building should be modified only where absolutely necessary; and secondly, the new space needed to be as flexible as possible.

The lower level of the existing space was a tunnel; a disused extension to the Madrid underground system built in 1945 – it had extreme dimensions; 107 metres in length yet only 8.5 metres wide. The upper level is a fine neoclassical arcaded space, originally built as an exhibition hall and part of the Spanish Government's complex of ministry buildings. To facilitate the connection between the train station underneath, and to create continuity between the conference/exhibition hall and the commuters, the designers decided to place the lecture theatre at basement station level. To create a link between the two levels they ingeniously broke through the floor of the upper space, an intervention that structurally compromised the arcaded hall.

A 500mm thick U-shaped concrete channel, 7.25 metres wide and 6.65 metres high was then inserted into the double-height space, which acted as a brace for the now-exposed sidewalls.

This incredible, top-lit room serves as a lecture theatre and conference space. The space between it and the walls allows services and utilities to be hidden; it structurally braces the walls of the building; and it resolves the tricky level changes between the arcade and the underground train station. When necessary, the theatre can be darkened by pulling a large heavy curtain around its walls, draping the cold, heavy concrete channel in a dark, velvety swathe of fabric. The exhibition hall is slotted deeper into the funnel and is where the entrance to the station has been placed. An extraordinary context has produced a brutally beautiful yet highly appropriate response.

Context and the interior

Top:
Lecture theatre
A dramatic three-dimensional relationship exists between the lecture theatre and the existing building.

Left:
Exterior
The COR-TEN® steel entrance box.

Above centre:
Plan
The plan shows the long, thin, subterranean space.

Above:
Section
The theatre is situated in the double-height space beneath the arches.

Introduction » Location » History » narrative

Important information
Each case study is introduced by name, location, date and designer.

Diagrams
Where possible, diagrams are used to illustrate the technical aspects of each project.

Captions
All captions carry a directional and title for easy reference.

How to get the most out of this book

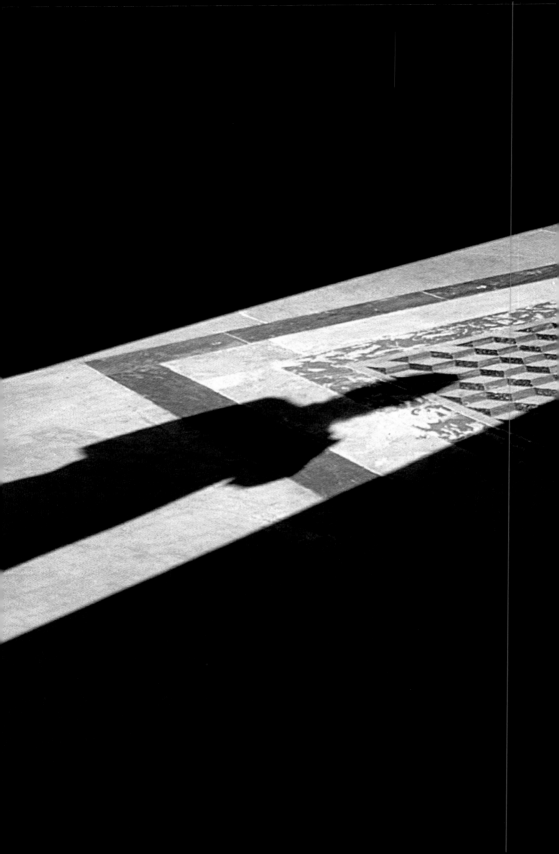

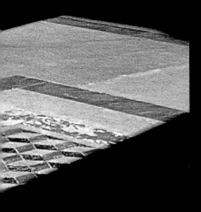

A building or interior occupies a unique situation; it is inherently connected to its site. This particular location or context contains a series of distinct qualities and possibilities. The designer can analyse and reveal these properties and use them to deepen and expand the quality of the interior. This chapter will analyse the way in which a building's context and surrounding environmental conditions might affect the design process.

Name:
Cathedral Museum
(see pp 022+023)

Location:
Lucca, Italy

Remodelled:
1993

Designer:
Pietro Carlo Pellegrini

The design process > Context and the interior

Properties of the existing site

This chapter will introduce the notion of studying the existing site and how the exploitation of its particular attributes can influence and inform the design of the interior. It will discuss how the different properties of the existing site can be examined and will investigate the different methods of exploring these.

Specific site issues

Before embarking on a project, most designers will start by uncovering a number of specific site issues. These issues are likely to vary from direct relationships with the immediate surroundings to more ephemeral connections with things further away, and the designer can develop the design based upon knowledge of these factors.

Analysis of the context

The exterior context can be an important and influential consideration. There are many site-specific situations that influence the shape and form of a building and subsequently affect the design of its interior. Such contextual factors can include aspect, orientation, topography, the patterns of street and roads, urban density, and its relationship with a significant landmark.

Analysis of the environment

The particular physical factors that are exerted on and experienced within a building will inevitably influence the design. Certain weather conditions need to be controlled; the rain and the wind can cause great discomfort and must therefore be eliminated. The long winter sunshine is very pleasant when admitted into an interior, but conversely, excessive solar gain in the height of summer is most unpleasant. Similarly, the orientation of an interior within its physical surroundings, and the use of particular materials will have a significant effect on the atmospheric qualities of a space and the feelings experienced by its users.

Sustainability issues

Sustainability is an issue that is becoming more influential in today's architectural designs. Factors such as low-energy use, low-impact and bioclimatic techniques will all need to be taken into account. Building reuse is a very sustainable approach; it reduces the amount of new natural resources necessary to construct a building. Other factors such as attitudes towards renewable and passive energy will also be examined.

The design process

Facing page:
Querini Stampalia Foundation, Venice, Italy (see pp 014+015).

It is through the discovery and understanding
of the properties of an existing site that the designer
can begin to connect, disconnect or reconnect the
space with its surroundings and the elements within
and imposed upon it. The designer can uncover
these qualities and use them as the basis for design.
All buildings and interiors are unique, in that the
contextual conditions for each are always different.

Properties of the existing site: Focus study 1

Name:
Querini Stampalia Foundation

Location:
Venice, Italy

Date:
1961–63

Designer:
Carlo Scarpa

Particular elements that are
present within a building's context
are often brought to the forefront
of architectural designs.

Carlo Scarpa allowed the water
naturally present within the
context of the Querini Stampalia
Foundation to have a direct
impact on his remodelling
of the ground floor and courtyard
garden of this sixteenth-century
Venetian palazzo. As such, the
design links the building with
the canal and thus ensures
that the visitor is very conscious
of the presence of water. Venice
is, after all, built on water, so
its buildings and people have
a strong relationship with it.

Scarpa began by clearing out
most of the fake columns and
wood panelling that were found
within the interior, and sought
to rediscover the character
and size of the original space.
He repositioned the front door,
placing it at the opposite end
of the façade from its original
position, and locating it to face
the Campiello, the little square
beside the Church of Santa
Maria Formosa. The new opening
is accessed by an elegant teak,
brass and steel bridge that
gracefully arches over the canal.

Scarpa designed two great steel
gates to the left of the bridge,
and these are open to the canal.
This allows water to flood into the
building at high tide. Within the
interior, diagonal steps allow the
visitor to descend to water level,
thus reinforcing the relationship
with the canal. This connection
is further emphasised beyond
the main gallery, in the courtyard
garden. This is an open room that
encloses a sequence of controlled
water channels placed around its
periphery. The water flows and
falls from one decorated concrete
trough to another, eventually
emptying into a circular basin.
The control and sequencing
of water, the main environmental
feature of Venice, is the vital
aspect of this interior space.

'Instead of viewing the water as a problem,
he chose to consider it as a resource, an opportunity,
a source of inspiration.'

Sergio Los

Facing page:
The gated room
The floodwater enters the space
and reconnects the visitor with
the canal.

Left:
The rear courtyard
The water flows through the
space, and is contained within
the concrete channel.

Below left:
Entrance bridge
The new modernist element
echoes many similar bridges
across the canal.

Below right:
Plan
Scarpa's intervention establishes
a link between the canal at
the front of the building and
the courtyard at the rear.

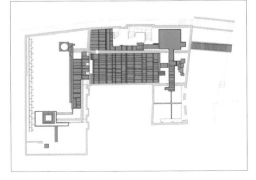

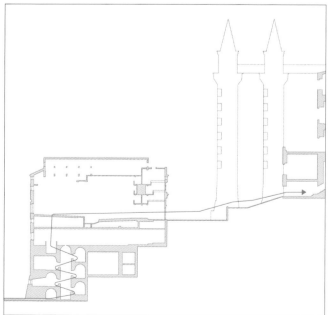

Above:
The historic city of Urbino
The view towards the palace. The car park can just be viewed to the right of the picture.

Left:
Section
The drawing shows the journey from the car park through the Mercatale Ramp to the palace.

'In my works in Urbino I have embedded all my experiences from around the world; and at the same time there always is a thread in my architectures that leads back to Urbino.'

Giancarlo De Carlo

Properties of the existing site: Focus study 2

Name:
The Mercatale Ramp

Location:
Urbino, Italy

Date:
1969–1983

Designer:
Giancarlo De Carlo

The reading of context is central to the process of creating a new interior space. The art of analysing an urban and existing building environment can create an understanding that is paramount to the shaping of a new situation.

Giancarlo De Carlo dedicated his life to the revitalisation of the city of Urbino. He was responsible for its new Law School (1966–68), Arts Faculty (1968–76), and Business School (1986–2002). All of the buildings were formed from an intimate understanding of the site and the rehabilitation of existing buildings and the spaces around them.

During the analysis of historic plans of the area, De Carlo discovered the existence of a stable and a passageway beneath the city walls and the theatre. This was originally designed to allow the duke to ride his horse from the stable, through the fortifications and into the much lower surrounding countryside. It was filled in to help support the foundations of the theatre.

De Carlo's discovery, excavation and subsequent rehabilitation of this passage revitalised a link between the lower level of the south-west part of the city and the upper-level streets and squares, thus creating a valuable link between the tourist car park and the centre.

The city of Urbino suffers from its own beauty and position as a popular tourist destination. The need to preserve its historical character and care for the numerous cultural monuments meant that the city planners effectively cut the historic core of the city from the surrounding suburbs. Cars and other forms of transport were removed from the centre, but a consequence of this was a degree of dislocation. Visitors had to alight in a massive car park beyond the city wall, and then begin the long journey around the walls to get to the centre. The passageway (or Mercatale Ramp) provides the perfect link; both convenient and charming, it is a magical way of beginning the exploration of the historic city.

Top:
The city walls
The difference in height between the car park and the city is clearly visible.

Above:
The theatre
The building grows out of the bastion wall.

A building or interior is naturally tied to its context. The site offers a series of unique conditions that are specific to that position only. These circumstances include the relationship with neighbouring spaces or buildings, the particular climatic conditions, the vista, view or orientation and factors such as history and previous function.

Specific site issues: Focus study 1

Name:
Wolfson Building, Trinity College

Location:
Cambridge, England

Date:
2006

Designer:
5th Studio

A building of radical and uncompromising qualities will often need remodelling with equally radical ambition.

This is the approach that 5th Studio has taken to work on this project. The Wolfson Building by Architects Co-Partnership was one of a series of brutalist buildings commissioned by Cambridge University in the 1960s and 70s. It is wilfully tough and formal, with a limited palette of exposed concrete, glass and brick. The form is an impressive symmetrical ziggurat of monumental proportions with a tunnel or arcade in the centre.

5th Studio was initially commissioned to upgrade the existing facilities, including the heating, lighting, environmental performance and circulation. The second phase involved the introduction of en suite bathrooms and development of the social spaces. The architects chose to slip a glass insertion into the open cavern at the heart of the existing building. The specific qualities of the existing site prompted the architects to design a strong yet reverential series of spaces that sheltered at the centre of the building. Two glass rooms were hung here, containing seminar and social spaces. A glass floor reinforces the precariousness of their position and reflective black glass allows light to penetrate into the central space, while also reflecting light into the circulation area. These glass additions mark the new entrance to the building in a manner that is both appropriately bold yet sufficiently respectful so as to not overawe the original. In this way, the qualities of the original 1970s build have been successfully re-interpreted for the twenty-first century.

Top:
The brutalist ziggurat
The new glass rooms are suspended from the top of the cavern.

Above:
Seminar room
Glass floors reinforce the perilous quality of the seminar rooms.

Above:
The hanging room
The social spaces hang
within the chasm.

Right:
**Section through the
centre of the building**
The glass insertion is
clearly visible.

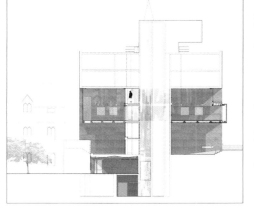

Properties of the existing site issues > **Specific site issues** > Analysis of the context

Specific site issues: Focus study 2

Name:
Oslo Town Hall

Location:
Oslo, Norway

Date:
1929–1950

Designer:
Arnstein Arneberg and
Magnus Poulsson

The designer may also choose to use the sociocultural context of a building to inform the remodelling of the interior.

Oslo Town Hall was designed in 1918, but world events meant that construction was not completed until 1950. The initial proposal was in keeping with the national Romantic style of Norwegian architecture, with medieval characteristics and details.

However, the time lapse in the construction gave the architects the opportunity to refine and develop their design and this turn of events resulted in a stripped-down and classically modern building. The town hall is situated next to the open waters of the natural harbour. Sitting in a hollow between the raised Akershus Fortress to the east and the mass of Victoria Terasse and the Ministry of Foreign Affairs to the west, the clean and functional brick building is composed of a regular, low, square block and is flanked by two imposing towers.

However, the interior is much more flamboyant. The main hall is decorated in an extravagant manner; the ceiling, walls and floor are covered with tiles, fabrics and murals depicting Nordic mythic scenes. These motifs carry through to the other rooms and depict romantic scenes from the country's history and development. As the backdrop to the yearly Nobel Peace Prize presentation, these make the setting particularly poignant, connecting the roots of Norwegian culture to modern life through decoration.

'Historically this connection is revealed through local materials and crafts, associations with the landscape, with historical events and with legends and myths.'

Steven Holl

Facing page:
Interior of the main hall
The sheer scale of the room is awe-inspiring.

Above:
Oslo City Hall
The brutal orthogonal building, as seen from the harbour.

Above right:
Side chamber
The side chamber is decorated with scenes from Nordic myths and legends.

Right:
The central hall
The richly decorated main space.

Properties of the existing site > Specific site issues > Analysis of the context

It is through an understanding and interpretation of the spirit of place and the particular contextual setting within which a building exists that the designer or architect can heighten, change and reactivate a space. An existing structure is bound to its setting; it has certain qualities that are unique only to that particular situation. The designer can analyse and use these found qualities as the starting point or basis for the next layer of construction.

Analysis of the context: Focus study 1

Name:
Cathedral Museum

Location:
Lucca, Italy

Date:
1993

Designer:
Pietro Carlo Pellegrini

A building's interior can reflect the landscape or cityscape in which it is situated.

The *Museo della Cattedrale di Lucca* is a microcosmic representation of the city in which it is located. The museum inhabits three buildings; a thirteenth-century townhouse, a sixteenth-century church and a seventeenth-century storehouse, all situated around the courtyard garden of the Piazza Antelminelli. The buildings exist as neighbours yet they are chronologically and stylistically different. The understanding of this unusual and diverse context provided the impetus for the design of the new museum.

The museum was designed to house artefacts from the nearby San Martino Cathedral. Pietro Pellegrini fused the three buildings together by carefully restoring each building – watchfully ensuring that the identity of each was left explicit – before sensitively stitching them together. This was achieved through the addition of a new timber, steel and glass circulation route, which cuts through new openings in the buildings. It serves to link all three buildings together and takes the visitor on a journey through and between the various rooms of the buildings.

The journey is made explicit by the retained scale and composition of the rooms; from the domestic spaces of the old house to the large worship hall of the church. The route is populated with religious artefacts, such as paintings and sculptures and the new openings through the series of spaces serve to frame views of these, thus providing the visitor with a visual clue as to the next stage of the journey. This winding path through the museum is a journey of delight and discovery.

Top:
Lucca Museum
The collection of buildings from Piazza Antiminelli.

Above:
View through the circulation route
Openings between the buildings provide the visitor with incidental views of the works of art in the gallery.

'As soon as the game or dialogue is understood the whole place begins to shake hands with you. It bursts all through the dull business of who did what and when and who did it first. We know who did it, it was a chap with a twinkle in his eye. This is the environment game and it's going on all around us.'

Gordon Cullen

Above:
Gallery space
The circulation route knits together the disparate buildings.

Right:
Plan
The plan clearly shows the three separate buildings.

'This is not simply a contextual gesture to the extent of blending in with the historic fabric. The opposite, rather, is true: the building completely reinterprets the existing plan, it challenges and redefines the pre-existing connections and hierarchies of the preserved historic centre, giving them new meaning and new dimensions as well as a new scale of urbanity.'

Münster City Library

Above:
The foyer
The noisy entrance is dynamic and busy, echoing its function.

Right:
Site plan
The library in context. Note the direct relationship to the church.

Analysis of the context: Focus study 2

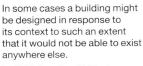

Name:
Münster City Library

Location:
Münster, Germany

Date:
1994

Designer:
Bolles + Wilson

In some cases a building might be designed in response to its context to such an extent that it would not be able to exist anywhere else.

In 1985 the city of Münster organised an architectural competition for the design of a library and museum. The building was to be located behind the fifteenth-century St Lamberti Church on one of the last-bombed sites. The competition was won by Bolles + Wilson, a fledgling practice based in London.

The new library (the museum was subsequently dropped from the competition) is profoundly contextual in that it has been developed as a response to its situation so much so that it could not exist in its current shape or form in any other place. The form and function of the building and its interior are a direct response to the urban pattern and fabric of the city. The shape of the building was dictated by the organisation of the existing streets, the windows positioned so that they admitted maximum amounts of light while still controlling any view through them and the activities positioned within the building to reflect the nature of the particular part of the city that they were adjacent to.

The important axial view through the site towards the church and its spire (a significant point of reference for Münster's history) prompted the development of a pedestrian passageway that runs centrally through the building. This street organises the building and its form.

The separation of the building into two allows for different zones within the library; the quiet reading and reference rooms are placed in the half-drum solitaire, while the noisier entrance, café, and public service areas reside in the main segment of the building. The two blocks are united twice; firstly in the basement, a wide horizontal space that contains the children's library and a small gallery, and then again at first-floor level. Here a bridge over the axial street links the book stacks and is guarded by the sliding information desk. Halfway across the bridge, above the axial route through the site, a small square window frames the view of the spire of the St Lamberti Church – the starting point for the original design of the building.

Top:
The axial route between the buildings
View to the Lamberti Church from within the linking bridge room in the library.

Above:
Reading room
The top-lit quiet space.

The particular climate, prevailing weather conditions and other background factors that a building or interior is subject to can all contribute to a building's internal environment. The use and control of these particular conditions can inform the design.

The designer may wish, for example, to take advantage of the sunlight available, or the interior might be orientated so that the primary spaces are situated away from noise, wind and rain.

Above:
Roof lights
Natural sunlight penetrates into the heart of the building.

Top to bottom:

Void through the house
The mezzanine bedrooms are pulled back to allow light into the living room.

Rear garden
The courtyard is treated as an outdoor room.

Axonometric of house
The double-height living area is directly connected to the heart of the building and the courtyard garden.

Analysis of the environment: Focus study 1

Name:
Adactus Housing

Location:
Preston, England

Date:
2006

Designer:
Architects Britch

The designer can make the best use of the prevailing physical conditions and limit the effects of those that are more problematic in order to create a comfortable and usable interior environment.

The typical English terrace house was constructed as cheap, quick and convenient housing for the working family of the nineteenth century. The design, which may have had slight regional variations, was basically three rooms downstairs and three up. On the ground floor was the parlour or best room at the front, the kitchen or family room at the back, with an extension or sometimes little more than a lean-to behind that, projecting into the backyard. Upstairs were two or three bedrooms with the later addition of a bathroom. These may have been deemed suitable in the nineteenth century, but the twenty-first century family lives in quite a different way. Architects Britch appreciated this when they were commissioned to update a series of individual terraces. They were also acutely aware of the environmental problems that existed within the site.

The approach taken was to move the prominent areas away from the street noise at the front of the house and reorientate them towards the peace and quiet at the back. As such, the kitchen and bathroom were moved to the front of the house and the living spaces became a large, partially double-height room at the rear, with direct access to the open outdoor space or 'living garden'. The bedrooms were placed on a mezzanine or balcony overlooking the living room, thus allowing natural sunlight to enter from roof lights and flood not only the bedrooms, but also to penetrate onto the ground floor. In doing this, the architects have controlled the house's immediate environment and equipped it for the modern family.

Below:
Concept sketch
The section shows relationship between light and living space.

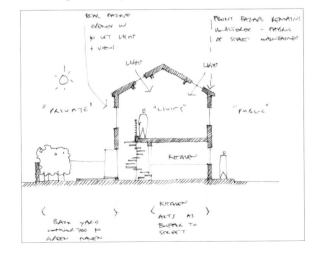

THIS GREAT COURT CELEBRA
THE BP SPECIAL EXHIBITION
micheLange-Lo
DRAWINGS
CLOSER TO THE MASTER
23 MARCH – 25 JUNE 2006
Room 5
Admission charge, timed entry.
Tickets from Box Office in the
Great Court and ticket desk
outside Room 5

Analysis of the environment: Focus study 2

Name:
Great Court, British Museum

Location:
London, England

Date:
2000

Designer:
Foster + Partners

An existing interior environment can be modified with a magnificent and expansive gesture.

The British Museum courtyard was once open and cluttered – little more than a convenient short cut and car park. Foster + Partners foresaw the advantages of turning this into a public area and decided to create a space that would be accessible to all visitors, containing service areas such as cafés and shops, and providing a place to meet and, most importantly, to slow the pace down and allow visitors to mentally adjust to the qualities of the museum.

The architects first of all cleared all the detritus and clutter from the courtyard, and then covered the area with an enormous, fully glazed, doughnut-shaped roof. This modified the climate, making it comfortable for visitors for the majority of the year. The roof keeps out the wind and rain, and prevents too much heat loss. Filters in the glass also alleviate the problem of excessive solar gain. The slightly concave roof is attached to the four façades of the courtyard and spans across the open courtyard to the central cylindrical reading room. It has no intermediate supports; the lattice structure is very delicate, yet strong. The complex geometry means that each triangular pane of glass is a slightly different size. The architects have created a living usable space by using an environmentally altering barrier to protect the courtyard.

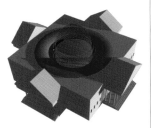

Facing page:
The Great Court
The new roof encourages public use of the newly enclosed space.

Left:
The old reading room
The fixings to the old building are minimal.

Below left:
Concept sketch
The doughnut shape of the glass roof is intrinsically strong.

Top:
The roof
The lattice of the roof appears to be very delicate.

Above:
Shadows on the courtyard wall
Filters in the glass alleviate the problems of excessive solar gain.

Analysis of the context > **Analysis of the environment** > Sustainability issues

The reuse of an existing building is an exercise in recycling that is both sustainable and much more energy efficient than most new-build architecture. As well as being extremely environmentally sensitive, reuse can also provide an antidote to the sterile architectural development that is prevalent in most city centres.

Sustainability issues: Focus study 1

Name:
Smithfield Buildings

Location:
Manchester, England

Date:
1998

Designer:
Stephenson Bell Architects

Developing and renewing old buildings is both sustainable and energy efficient and can breathe new life into an area that has become run-down or out of fashion.

In the Northern Quarter, an area of Manchester set aside in the recent urban regeneration for creative communities, developers Urban Splash acquired the 1904 Affleck and Brown department store. They commissioned Stephenson Bell to remodel the building into flats and retail spaces for the designers, artists and musicians who were keen to live in the area.

The additions and accretions were stripped away from the nine existing buildings that made up the site, and the remnants of a courtyard were discovered. This informed the subsequent diagram of the design for the new building. The designers proposed that retail units should occupy the ground-floor level on all four sides of the building, with apartments stacked around the edge of the courtyard. Access to the apartments is through a triple-height entrance space just off Tib Lane, the quietest street surrounding the building.

A staircase leads to the first-floor courtyard, which forms a glazed winter garden and from which all of the 81 apartments are accessed. This courtyard is landscaped and treated as a public space for the occupants of the building. It is constructed in a robust exterior fashion with steel walkways and solid timber decking. It also houses the services for the apartments, such as water, electricity and air extraction. As such, the courtyard has a dual function; it is both a public space and an area for housing private services.

Because of the idiosyncrasies of the existing buildings, the apartments vary greatly. Some have external private balconies, terraces, or access to a roof garden; and the top-floor flats have roof lights. The designers have successfully reused what was a much-loved Manchester landmark building with a varied and interesting history, and have reinvented it in a sustainable and sympathetic manner, as a place for modern inner-city living.

Above:
Building exterior
Retail spaces occupy the ground floor level while residential apartments are situated above.

Below left:
Entrance
The triple-height hallway leads to the first floor winter garden.

Below right:
Winter garden
This multi-functional space is used for circulation and services, as well as a place for meeting and relaxing.

Bottom left:
Plan
Flats are arranged around the central winter garden.

Bottom right:
Section
The first-floor courtyard has a direct relationship to the flats and the entrance area.

'The continued use and development of existing buildings is fundamentally sustainable. Its aim is to maximise the overall lifetime of buildings. It ensures that the effort and investment that was required to originally erect a building can be utilised for as long as possible into the present and future.'

**Johannes Cramer and
Stefan Breitling**

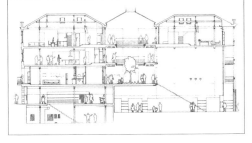

Analysis of the environment > **Sustainability issues**

Left:
Aerial view
The buildings are arranged to minimise shadows.

Sustainability issues: Focus study 2

Name:
Beddington Zero Energy Development (BedZED)

Location:
London, England

Date:
2001

Designer:
Bill Dunster Architects

New-build projects provide excellent opportunities for designs to incorporate sustainable, low-energy strategies.

BedZED is a mixed-use, high-density development of 82 town houses, maisonettes and apartments designed as a sustainable community in the London Borough of Sutton. It also includes workspaces for about 20 businesses, an organic café and shop, nursery, healthy living centre and even a village green. The development is built on an old disused sewage works and has transformed the site into a model of urban sustainability.

The scheme is an ambitious development, bringing together committed designers Bill Dunster Architects, developers BioRegional Development Group and the Peabody Trust, in order to realise the Government's definition of a sustainable, environmental and social housing community.

Sustainability is most evident in the low-energy strategies used in the construction process; the sourcing and transporting of materials and the impact on future energy use when the houses are in use. Everything, from the orientation of the houses on the site, to the triple glazing and insulation technology, has been designed to make the least possible impact on the environment and to be as energy efficient as possible. The buildings avoid any dependence on inefficient electrical and mechanical systems in their design and aim to ensure that there is zero fossil fuel usage when inhabited. Instead, they depend upon biomass for their energy.

Local economic sustainability is promoted by the use of local networks and suppliers for food and services, and recycled material is used where possible – minimising impact on all energy use. The form and fabric of the building has been carefully designed to maximise natural energy while minimising waste. The houses are arranged as terraces in order to minimise shading and maximise solar gain, allowing heat gain and energy storage and also saving on artificial lighting by making the houses as light as possible. Cross-ventilation allows the apartments to stay cool in summer and in winter the high insulation values of each apartment retain heat. Black water and grey water is recycled and used for water-saving toilets, washing machines and dishwashers. Even the buildings themselves are constructed from high-grade steel that was salvaged from a demolished building nearby and transported to the site.

BedZED is considered by many to be the future model for sustainable development in housing.

The design process

Above:
Roof scape
The novelty chimney cowls.

Far left:
BedZED entrance
The materials are connected to
the landscape.

Left:
BedZED terrace
The south-facing façade absorbs
as much sunlight as possible.

BDa ZEDfactory
Bill Dunster Architects ZEDfactory Ltd (BDa ZEDfactory)
is an award-winning practice, specialising in
low energy, low environmental impact buildings.
Renewable energy devices and passive energy
features are an inherent part of their design thinking.

Analysis of the environment > **Sustainability issues**

Context and the interior

An interior occupies a specific place. It has its own identity and a distinct relationship with its surroundings, involving not just the building it occupies, but also its immediate neighbours and things more remote.

The perception, character and scale of a particular building or place can be influenced by its *genius loci*, or spirit or identity of place. The interior is just a small element within a huge collage of different points and references. This chapter looks at the ways in which the relationships between these might affect the design of the interior. The factors that form the setting for the interior and the terms in which it can be understood, such as its relationship with location, history, external elements, the transition between inside and outside and movement through the building's spaces and surroundings, will all be very important tools for the designer.

Name:
Galleria Nazionale
(see pp 058+059)

Location:
Parma, Italy

Date:
1987

Designers:
Guido Canali

Location

The location in which the existing building or space is situated is inevitably influential. The interior has a relationship with what is immediately around it, whether this is a dense urban context or an open landscape. It also is part of its own context; relationships exist within the interior space, whether these are three-dimensional connections between particular levels or horizontal links across a space or series of spaces.

History + narrative

The time at which a building was constructed and the changes that have been made to it will have great influence upon its design. A space that was constructed for a specific purpose will have particular and precise characteristics; it is these that our pluralistic and postmodern society enjoys exposing and celebrating. The patina of time is generally regarded as a sign of beauty and worth, and the revelation can add to the joy of experiencing a space. Reference to the history and narrative of a building can be regarded as a design tool of great worth.

External connections

Connections between the interior and an exterior feature can form the basis of interesting designs. These connections can be made with things that are both near and far, particular landmarks may be referred to and opportunities for counterpoint and balance can be explored.

Threshold

The transition between outside and inside is very important to the designer, not just for reasons of access, but also because it offers an opportunity to make connections. These will be made at the moment of entrance and also through openings within the walls of the building. They also offer the designer the chance to physically and psychologically change the attitude of the visitor or occupier of the space.

Visual connections

The exploitation of the outlook of a space can offer the designer great opportunities; the designer can create situations that take advantage of a spectacular situation or vista. But the designer must also acknowledge the problems incurred by the direction in which the space is facing – there may be difficulty with excessive solar gain, a prevailing wind or an unpleasant view – whatever difficulties or delights are presented by the particular aspect, they must be addressed.

Movement

Movement through a building can be very straightforward (for example, a simple series of discrete and uncomplicated spaces) or it can become a narrative. It can expose and reveal the story of the building. The complex three-dimensional qualities of the interior can be communicated through movement.

Above:
Bar Ten, Glasgow, Scotland (see
pp 038+039 and 160+161).

The particular place in which an interior exists can exert great influence on the design. A bright, open situation may prompt the designer to conceive of a dark and enclosed interior, which would provide strong contrast between interior and exterior. Conversely, the designer might choose to reflect the qualities of the space, creating a continuity with the location. The designer can allow the location to influence the design of the interior in the way that they choose.

Above:
The interior of the bar
The finishes have a robust, exterior-like quality.

Right:
Entrance
The fully glazed façade opens the bar on to the alleyway.

Location: Focus study 1

Name:
Bar Ten (see also pp 160+161)

Location:
Glasgow, Scotland

Date:
1991

Designer:
Ben Kelly Design

A dense urban situation is a common condition for the redesigned interior. The buildings may be listed and therefore cannot be changed, but the interior will offer many opportunities for creative and contemporary interventions.

In their approach to the design of Bar Ten, Ben Kelly Design opened up the space and liberated it from the surrounding tight and constraining environment. It is located down a narrow and shadowy alleyway, discreetly hidden away from the busy shoppers on Princes Square, Glasgow's main retail area. Ben Kelly Design decided to completely open the façade of the bar by fully glazing the front elevation. This act provides the interior with a very European feel; it is almost part of the street. The name, Bar Ten, is written in huge letters across the window to filter views in or out. At night this offers some protection to the visitors to the bar but during the day this also allows natural daylight to illuminate the interior.

The organisation of the bar is conceived as a sequence of spaces or experiences that start at the busy shopping street and finish within the tranquillity of the bar. The series of gradually diminishing spaces is emphasised by the compact quality of the interior. The visitor connects with the interior while still being outside. The finishes are robust and uncompromising; they have an exterior quality, thus reinforcing the idea that the street and the bar are linked.

The muscular structure of the existing building was preserved and then exposed. The three large existing columns were retained, and the counter placed in front of these, so that the open public space remains uncluttered. The floor and the bar-front are both finished in dark terrazzo and thus not only appear to be connected to and have the same sense of solidity as the outside, but also appear to share the same robust, exterior characteristics. Other elements, such as the countertop, the foot-rail and the air-extraction systems are positioned to reinforce this continuation; each is long and encourages the eye to move into the depths of the space, thus completing the journey from the hectic main street to the serene interior.

The double height allows the space to breathe, yet the mixture of integral fixed objects and furniture, and the palette of rugged and industrial materials emphasise the intensity of the compact space and refer to Glasgow's tough spirit and mercantile heritage.

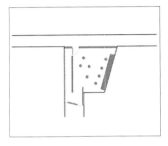

Top:
Concept sketch
The designer's concept sketch shows the direct relationship between the interior, alleyway and shopping street.

Above:
Plan
Movement is paramount within the design.

Introduction > **Location** > History + narrative

'The building that is to be remodelled is also part of its own context. The quality of the individual spaces, the relationship of one room with another and of each floor with the one below or above, the positions of the doors, the windows and the circulation areas all contribute to the intricate composition of the existing building.'

Graeme Brooker and Sally Stone

Location: Focus study 2

Name:
Architectural
Documentation Centre

Location:
Madrid, Spain

Date:
2004

Designer:
Aparicio + Fernández-Elorza

Sites that have unusual or extraordinary characteristics can lead the designer to create an equally remarkable interior. Within this project, the quite extreme qualities of the site and its existing structures have led to a daring and innovative intervention by the architects in order to realise the necessary requirements of the project.

The Architectural Documentation Centre was formed within the long arcade of a disused building and the underground platform below it, in the Nuevos Ministerios district. Two main principles guided the design: firstly, the existing building should be modified only where absolutely necessary, and secondly, the new space needed to be as flexible as possible.

The lower level of the existing space was a tunnel, a disused extension to the Madrid underground system built in 1945 – it had extreme dimensions; 107 metres in length yet only 8.5 metres wide. The upper level is a fine neoclassical arcaded space, originally built as an exhibition hall and part of the Spanish Government's complex of ministry buildings. To facilitate the connection between the train station underneath, and to create continuity between the conference/exhibition hall and the commuters, the designers decided to place the lecture theatre at basement station level. To create a link between the two levels they ingeniously broke through the floor of the upper space, an intervention that structurally compromised the arcaded hall.

A 500mm thick U-shaped concrete channel, 7.25 metres wide and 6.65 metres high was then inserted into the double-height space, which acted as a brace for the now-exposed sidewalls.

This incredible, top-lit room serves as a lecture theatre and conference space. The space between it and the walls allows services and utilities to be hidden; it structurally braces the walls of the building; and it resolves the tricky level changes between the arcade and the underground train station. When necessary, the theatre can be darkened by pulling a large heavy curtain around its walls, draping the cold, heavy concrete channel in a dark, velvety swathe of fabric. The exhibition hall is slotted deeper into the tunnel and is where the entrance to the station has been placed. An extraordinary context has produced a brutally beautiful yet highly appropriate response.

Context and the interior

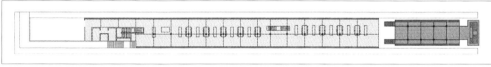

Top:
Lecture theatre
A dramatic three-dimensional relationship exists between the lecture theatre and the existing building.

Left:
Exterior
The COR-TEN® steel entrance box.

Above centre:
Plan
The plan shows the long, thin, subterranean space.

Above:
Section
The theatre is situated in the double-height space beneath the arches.

The previous function or use of a building or space can exert an influence over the redesign; the memory of an earlier life or existence can bring about wonderful interactions and relationships within remodelled buildings. The presence of the past can inform and liberate the future.

History + narrative: Focus study 1

Name:
National Museum of Roman Art

Location:
Merida, Spain

Date:
1989

Architect:
Rafael Moneo

The preservation of ruins or remains, which are often of cultural and historical importance, can provide the impetus for the design of surrounding spaces and structures.

The town of Merida was founded in 25BC and was so influential in the Holy Roman Empire that it was regarded as the capital of Lusitania. A number of culturally and technologically important structures were constructed in the city, including an ampitheatre and arena and a spectacular aqueduct. Much of the new town of Merida is constructed directly on top of the Roman city, and the National Museum of Roman Art is no exception. In fact, before construction could begin, archaeological investigations revealed the presence of a Roman village, a necropolis, part of the main Roman road and a section of the San Lazaro aqueduct on the site. The preservation of these ruins – recognition of the previous life of the site – formed an important part of the strategy for the redesign of the museum.

The grain, or predominant street patterns, of the new and old cities are at quite different angles. Moneo exploited this and actually made it a feature within the construction. The basement was actually built over the exposed excavated remains of buildings. The museum is constructed from Roman bricks and is realised as a series of monumental Roman arches that rise from the basement ruins. These arches carefully climb over the ruined walls of the old Roman settlement. The basement is dimly lit and is incredibly atmospheric as the rigid rhythm of the new walls contrasts with the ruined qualities of the old.

The building is made up of two main parts, notionally separated by the outline footprint of the ruined Roman road. They are connected by a wide walkway that floats over the outline of the old road and that acts to both separate and link both sides of the museum and provide the main circulation route through the space.

The old and the new are both strong and monumental, and although built from the same material using a similar language, they contrast and complement each other.

Top:
The ground floor gallery
The bricks are typically Ancient Roman – long and thin.

Above:
Main hall
The top-lit space is ordered and controlled by the series of walls and arches.

Context and the interior

'...even in historic times documents were not always available, and buildings (monuments, vernacular constructions, and public works) are themselves important texts, often providing the first and most lasting impression of a culture.'

Jorge Silvetti

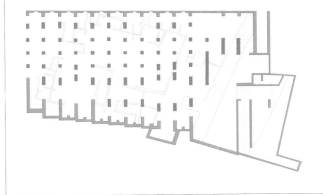

Above:
The basement
The new structure straddles the old ruins.

Left:
Plan
The order of the new building is juxtaposed against the grain of the Roman remains.

History + narrative: Focus study 2

Name:
Museum of Childhood

Location:
Bethnal Green, England

Date:
2003–2006

Designer:
Caruso St John Architects

Buildings that have had an unusual and varied history can provide the designer with many exciting tools with which to approach the design.

The Museum of Childhood building was originally constructed in 1857 as the South Kensington Museum on the site of the Victoria and Albert Museum (its parent institution) in London. It was built from the profits of the Great Exhibition of 1851 and, in some ways, resembled Paxton's building; three partially glazed barrel-vaulted aisles are supported by a cast-iron frame. When in 1866 the V&A built a more permanent and dignified building, the original was dismantled and reassembled ten miles to the east in Bethnal Green, where it has remained ever since. The majority of the original building was reused, but new exterior walls of red brick were constructed to replace the first corrugated iron ones.

The first phase of the twenty-first century remodelling involved the cleaning and restoration of the main structure and the repair of the fish-scale pattern mosaic marble floor of the main hall. New furniture and colour-coordinated display cabinets were then arranged to complement the space and engage the visitors in a dialogue with activities and the objects around them.

The new brick façades were never completely satisfactory; the 1866 budget constraints meant that they were not as welcoming, elaborate or spacious as the architect had originally intended. The second phase of the remodelling project addressed this; Caruso St John has constructed a new loggia, which creates the much needed entrance foyer. The new space contains the lobby, a new gallery space and also offices and services.

The new entrance loggia is orthogonally modern and contrasts strongly with the Victorian building. But it is constructed from coloured, patterned stonework – quartzite, various porphyries and shades of Ancaster limestone – laid with precision by the same traditional masons who worked on the restoration of Hawksmoor's Christ Church in Spitalfields. This serves as a reference to the existing mosaics in the museum, the original 1866 proposal and the Victorians' regard for renaissance.

The intended third phase of the project will move the existing offices from the south to make way for a café and garden and engage a neighbouring church, thus connecting the building back to its community.

The various phases of the remodelling of the Museum of Childhood seek to 'complete' the building and develop the started but as yet unfinished dialogue with its context and its history.

Context and the interior

Facing page:
The new extension
The new foyer adopts
the intended position of the
original porch.

Below:
The central hall
The designers have reordered
the interior.

'We're trying to start to express more formally
the idea that interpretation is a very powerful thing.
Interpretation of tradition has always been how
you made art and architecture.'

Adam Caruso

Above:
Wall panel
The tessellated design reflects
the mosaic pattern of the
ground floor.

Relationships between the interior and the exterior
of a building are very important. The inside is not
an autonomous space without any connection to what
is happening around it. Interiors can be designed to
have a significant bond with both things and people
beyond the exact boundaries of the immediate space.

External connections: Focus study 1

Name:
Retti candle shop and
Schullin jewellery shop

Location:
Vienna, Austria

Date:
1964–65 and 1972–74

Architect:
Hans Hollein

It is common, particularly in retail and shop environments, for the interior to hold strong connections to the street on which it is located.

Hans Hollein has created two distinct retail spaces, both of which are similar in that they are economic in their use of space, distinct in their material qualities, and highly sophisticated in their relationships with the street.

The Retti candle shop is situated in one of Vienna's most exclusive shopping streets, the Kohlmarkt. A brushed aluminium screen deliberately conceals the shop window. Punched into the centre of this screen is a T-shaped doorway and a glass door allows axial views into the heart of the shop. On either side of this entrance are small display cases, which slightly protrude from the sheer face of the screen. The display boxes focus directly and tightly on the objects on show, thus accentuating their value, while deliberately removing any spatial relationship between the shop window and the shop. The passing shopper is not overwhelmed with a dazzling shop display; rather they are intrigued by the sense of distance and preciousness glimpsed within. The doorway, like the façade, is lined with aluminium, so the actual moment of entry is extended far beyond the usual shopping experience. In this way, the shop's relationship with the street has become exaggerated and the viewer's gaze has become concentrated through the strength of the shop opening and the focus of the axis.

The Juwelier Schullin is also in Vienna and is, again, a narrow site with a small rectangular interior. Hollein once more uses a screen to reduce the sheer size of the shop window, allowing the shopper's gaze to concentrate on the jewellery and accentuating the worth of the displayed objects. The black-brown polished Baltic granite façade is 'cracked' and then inlaid with polished brass and steel. This fissure alludes to the depth of the screen façade and speaks of the geological process of excavating the precious stones that are now polished and held within the interior. Cunningly, the fracture also contains the air conditioning extraction and inlet pipes. The split runs the height of the new façade and also the depth of the new shop front. It finally rests on the brass plate of the door, drawing the eye from the exterior to the front door and into the interior. The relationship between the inside and the outside is both reduced and concentrated, thus accentuating the nature of the jewellery box and the preciousness of the objects inside.

Context and the interior

'Hans Hollein [is] a master of his profession – one who with wit and eclectic gusto draws upon the traditions of the New World as readily as upon those of the Old. An architect who is also an artist…'

Citation from the Pritzker Jury, Pritzker Architecture Prize Laureate 1985

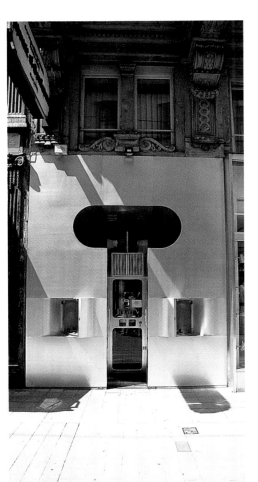

Left:
The Retti candle shop
The façade seems to be extruded from the interior.

Above:
The Schullin jewellery shop
The façade seems to be carved from rock.

Facing page:
Façade detail
The crevasse within the fascia is exquisitely finished.

'An outdoor space becomes a special outdoor room when it is well enclosed with the walls of the building, walls of foliage, columns, trellis, and sky; and when the outdoor room together with an interior room, forms a virtually continuous living area.'

Christopher Alexander

External connections: Focus study 2

Name:
STUK Performing Arts Centre

Location:
Leuven, Belgium

Date:
2002

Designer:
Neutelings Riedijk Architects

An established routeway or shared space can serve to link a building with its surroundings, as well as with other buildings around it.

STUK has been carefully inserted into a university collection of old buildings on a steep hillside in the town centre of Leuven. Work on this project involved a complex combination of demolition, reuse and new-build. The original turn-of-the-century building facing the street was retained and remodelled to house the theatre, dance studios, a café and the centre's reception. A large and simple steel sign was placed in front of it to announce the new use to the street. A number of unimportant buildings at the back of the site were demolished and a series of new buildings carefully dropped into the awkwardly enclosed site.

The arrangement of new and old buildings is based around a series of existing courtyards, allowing both the new and the old to connect together as well as serving to link everything throughout the site. The new complex has become a 'city within the city'; an architectural promenade of linked rooms, courtyards or spaces, which each have their own distinct atmosphere. The designers have deliberately ensured that amongst this patchwork of buildings every part of the complex has access to a courtyard. And so, the spaces between the buildings are as important as the spaces within them – each building has its own door on to a courtyard, thus reinforcing the policy of the arts centre as a series of formal and informal rooms for experimentation and interaction.

During the day the spaces are actively busy, but at night and in good weather the courtyards become more social spaces. The large wide steps in the courtyards not only provide access to the upper floors of buildings but can also be used as seating to watch outdoor performances and screened films. The unusual topography of the hilly site has influenced the stepped layers of the buildings and spaces, and contributed to the complex layers of the museum.

This project is very typical of the Dutch concept of bigness, the idea that there is very little visual difference between a building (or interior) when it is viewed close up or from a distance. The detailing is very carefully controlled, the junctions are minimal; materials are designed to appear as pure clean planes with little or no interference or breaks. Much of Neutelings Riedijk's work is like this: modernism taken to an extreme – the buildings are the same from wherever they are viewed. It is a style in stark contrast to the more interpretive methods practised by designers such as Scarpa, Kelly or Zumthor.

Context and the interior

Facing page:
Signage
The bold, graphic element signals the street façade of the building.

Above:
Vertical circulation
The stairs are bold and dynamic elements within the interior.

Above:
The courtyard
The façade of each building opens onto this space.

Below:
The animated courtyard space
The courtyard provides a great social space for films and gatherings.

Above left:
Concept sketch
The building is a collection of distinct elements.

Above right:
Plan
The 'carpet' of programme.

The relationship between the inside and the outside of a building is generally at its most extreme at the threshold. For example, the front door of a building will provide the moment of change between the public exterior and the private interior. It is at this point that a psychologically and almost unconscious change occurs; the visitor generally becomes quieter, movement slows down and materials and finishes within the building tend to reflect this smaller internal focus. The designer can prolong and exploit this moment by extending the transitional point, by ensuring that the visitor or user is aware of the transition from public street to the private interior.

Threshold: Focus study 1

Name:
The Haçienda nightclub

Location:
Manchester, England

Date:
1982

Designer:
Ben Kelly Design

The designer can promote movement from the exterior, to and through the interior by employing a device known as the 'architectural promenade'. This encourages the visitor or occupier to experience the journey as a series of different but linked spaces.

In 1980s Manchester, nightclubs didn't exist. Instead there were 'discos', which were glamorous, pretentious places with severe door policies. Then Ben Kelly designed the Haçienda. It was a three-dimensional version of the owners, Factory Records: innovative and visually outrageous, and it created a new type of venue for music, drinking, eating and, most importantly, dancing. The club was in an enormous, old, converted yachting showroom; it looked like a warehouse and it was nothing like a disco.

Within the Haçienda a most theatrical architectural promenade is used. The presence of the club on the street was almost non-existent; the clubber would pass through a small dark door into a tight lobby, from there into a slightly larger area and then:

'...into a massive cathedral-like space which heightens and magnifies this experience, you become overwhelmed once you're in there, it takes you over.'

This is typical of Ben Kelly Design's work, where movement is linear and the design is very much about the movement and circulation of people through the interior. Spaces are designed in series, as a progression of scenes for the user to inhabit. Each is connected to the last through the themed use of materials, textures and colours but every one with a distinct and identifiable atmosphere.

Context and the interior

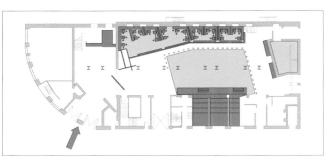

Facing page:
Interior of the club
The cavernous, warehouse-like dance floor as viewed from the foyer.

Above:
The dance floor
The entrance arch can be seen beyond the sprung floor.

Left:
The stage
The stage embodies the bold, industrial imagery of the nightclub.

Below left:
Plan
The drawing shows the journey through the interior.

Threshold: Focus study 2

Name:
Comme des Garçons
perfume shop

Location:
Paris, France

Date:
1998

Designer:
Future Systems (exterior)
Rei Kawakubo &
Takao Kawasaki (interior)

The designer can extend the journey between inside and outside so that it is experienced as a series of gradual steps or episodes. Conversely, the revelation of the interior at the point of the threshold can be a surprise or even a shock.

Future Systems, Rei Kawakubo and Takao Kawasaki successfully created an experience of this kind in their design of the Comme des Garçons perfume shop.

The shop occupies the ground floor of an apartment block. The outside was quite crudely treated; the arched openings of the existing building were cleaned and any existing doors and windows removed. Huge square panels of laminated glass were then unceremoniously attached to the stone façade. These vast pieces of glass were not cut to the size of the openings, but were conceived of as a transparent wall or veil, designed to fit against the face of the building, to completely cover all of the ground-floor façade and butt up against the cornice. A bright pink film was placed between the laminates of glass, so that both the walls of the white Portland stone building and the interior of the shop appear to be pink.

But at the threshold, this rose-tinted interior is exposed as a trick; the inside of the shop is stark and white. The display shelves are constructed from bright white painted steel and are brilliantly lit, thus maximising the contrast between the inside and outside experience. The items for sale are kept to the absolute minimum and these are displayed in two deep slots cut into the curved steel display element.

'My shops are conceived for people who get energy from wearing these clothes, who like taking risks,' says Rei Kawakubo – certainly they would need to be brave to cross this dramatic and contrasting threshold.

Above:
The shop façade
The rose-coloured glass completely covers the front of the shop.

Right:
Entrance to the shop
The fixings are minimal and do not disrupt the planar qualities of the glass.

Below:
Concept sketch
The shop is designed as two juxtaposed elements.

Threshold

The point of transition between inside and outside space is often defined as the threshold between these two spaces. Any doorway could really be described as a threshold and the word is often used as a metaphor for the beginning of an adventure.

An interior often has a relationship with the outside world. It will usually make reference not only to itself, but also to things further away. Windows and other openings offer views and can make connections with things close up and with things more remote.

Above:
The box in context
The box is a dramatic element within a breathtaking scene.

Visual connections: Focus study 1

Name:
GucklHupf

Location:
Mondsee, Austria

Date:
1993

Designer:
Hans Peter Wörndl

Occasionally the designer can work to create an interior that will edit and frame views of its surroundings.

'Gucken: to watch, observe, Hupfen: to hop.'

A very strange structure, designed for the 1993 Festival of Regions in northern Austria, established a rapport with its surrounding landscape. The theme of the festival was 'strangeness', and a series of performances, exhibitions, workshops and art installations were produced to explore that idea. On a hillside overlooking the Mondsee Lake, Wörndl and two friends conceived and built a pavilion dedicated to strangeness. They decided not to use conventional plans, but mostly made it up as they went along. They would change the details as they built it but never lost sight of the initial concept; the finished object had to embody the ambiguities inherent within the theme of the festival.

The two-storey wooden pavilion was designed as a place for observation and meditation. The 4 x 6 x 7-metre building was constructed from a wooden frame clad with marine ply panels. A series of pulleys, ties and levers opened and closed these panels, so the pavilion could be completely open or closed, or anything in-between.

When inside, the occupant could edit and frame views across the stunning landscape by treating the walls as giant picture frames, to be arranged at their pleasure. The viewer had control over their relationship with the surrounding landscape, while hiding within the protection of the small, contorting structure.

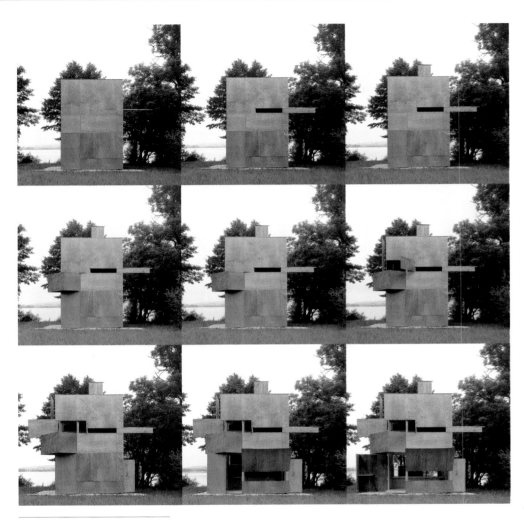

Above:
GucklHupf
The sequence of unfolding.

Top to bottom:

View from the balcony
The landing protrudes
precariously from the bell tower.

Internal view from the balcony
The language of the insertion
is industrial and robust.

The circular staircase
The three stages of the staircase
are clearly visible.

Above:
Summit of the staircase
The final ascent is dramatic
and dangerous.

Facing page:
Sketch section
The staircase is constructed
in three parts.

Context and the interior

Narrative

Architectural narrative is a device that describes the story of a building. It is usually a series of events that gradually reveal the nature or character of a space, building or complex. The designer may wish to convey many different things, such as the history, geology or geography, the brand or identity, or the relationship with other elements.

Above left:
Interior of the chamber
The thousands of glass stones light up the dark chamber.

Above:
The courtyard
The small cage at the front of the space contains the only view of the river.

The natural world within which
a building exists plays a vital role
in defining the atmosphere and
qualities of an interior. Environmental
control within a space need not
be a process that is simply handled
by an engineer. It can be considered
an intrinsic part of the design process.
The well-designed interior can take
advantage of particular environmental
conditions, such as climate, light and
temperature, and manipulate them to
the advantage of the space. The choice
of materials and the manipulation of
an interior's orientation and aspect can
also play an important role in the feel
and comfort of the interior.

Name:
H2O Expo, freshwater pavilion
(see pp 072+073)

Location:
Neeltje Jans, The Netherlands

Date:
1997

Designer:
NOX Architecture

Climate

The climate will have a direct influence upon the quality of the interior. Necessary measures always have to be taken to ensure that the occupied spaces are adequately comfortable. These measures include controlling the temperature, regulating the amount of heat admitted and keeping out rain, wind, snow and excessive heat.

Light

The control and manipulation of natural light can create exquisite or dramatic atmospheres. The quality of natural light can vary with the seasons: the long, watery, winter sun is both welcoming and warming as it penetrates deep into the heart of a space, but the intensity of the high, bright, summer blaze can be uncomfortable, thus creating the need for shade.

Temperature

Humans are only able to live comfortably within a very narrow band of different temperature levels. For this reason, architects have always had to be aware of temperature control and user comfort within their designs. Such mechanisms have been highly sophisticated since Ancient Roman times and often involve the capture and control of natural resources.

Orientation

The designer can manipulate the position of the space or building, turning the main spaces towards favourable conditions and away from unattractive ones, whether this is the sun, particular weather conditions or a response to contextual features. This can often significantly alter both the spirit and physical conditions of an interior.

View/aspect

The space can face, or be orientated towards a particular physical landmark or view: a response to the aspect.

Materials

The materials that a space is constructed from will have a large effect on the internal environment. Physical factors such as acoustics, temperature and light can all be altered in this way. Materials can also help create atmosphere, and can link a space with its context.

Facing page:
The Alhambra (The Red Palace), Granada, Spain (see pp 074+075).

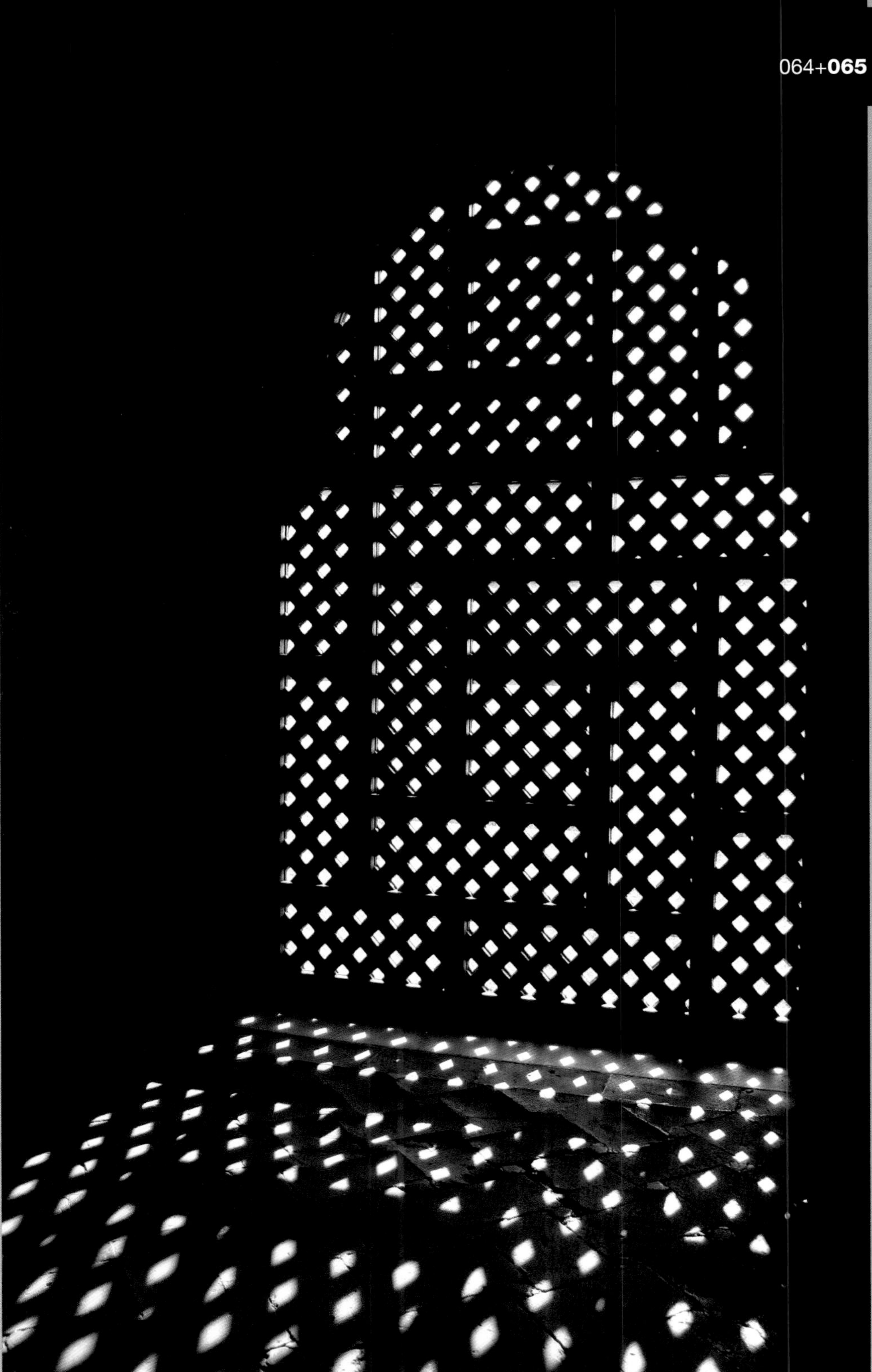

The weather conditions within which a building or interior exists can influence the quality and comfort of a space. A room that is stuffy, too hot or, conversely, too cold is uncomfortable and difficult to live or work in. The designer is often presented with the difficult task of balancing exquisite design with user comfort and the methods of doing this are becoming increasingly sophisticated and environmentally sustainable. The final section of this book looks at these strategies in greater detail.

Below:
The dome at night
The spiralling ramp and inverted cone are clearly visible.

Above:
Interior of the dome
The triple-glazed transparent dome offers dramatic views across the rooftops of Berlin. Note the moveable sunscreen on the left-hand side.

Left:
Section
The direct relationship between the dome, the cone and the debating chamber is clearly visible.

Environment and the interior

'The spectacular parliamentary chamber forms the heart of the building. Above rises a dome, not a restoration of the one which burned in 1938, but certainly incorporating memories of the past.'

Kenneth Powell

Climate: Focus study 1

Name:
Reichstag dome

Location:
Berlin, Germany

Date:
1999

Designer:
Foster + Partners

Design is often a fine balance of exploiting particular environmental conditions while also providing protection against them.

The Reichstag, or New German Parliament building, is a well known and easily identifiable building amongst the Berlin skyline. The glass dome, rising from the centre of the building, is synonymous with German reunification and as such is a symbol of amity and democracy. The dome was constructed by Foster + Partners in 1999 as an integral part of the renovation and refurbishment of a building that had been disused for fifty years, so that it could once again become the centre of government.

The original building, constructed in 1894 by Paul Wallot, an architect from Frankfurt, was designed in an Italianate or neo-Renaissance style and was, even then, dominated by a large glass cupola at the top of the building. The building has had a turbulent history: it was severely damaged twice; once in 1933 by a fire that enabled the National Socialists to suspend democratic law and then seize more power, and then by the advancing Soviet army, who virtually demolished the building in the final Battle of Berlin at the end of the Second World War. The building was partially and unsympathetically restored in the 1960s but was still left empty and deemed unsuitable for governmental use. However, German reunification prompted a competition to be organised to remodel the Reichstag to house the new German Bundestag.

Foster + Partners won the competition with a design that reinstated the cupola as a symbolic glass dome – a glowing representation of the democratic process. The dome houses a magnificent spiral ramp that allows visitors a long, elevated promenade around the structure and an uninterrupted view across the city.

It also provides a glimpse of the democratic processes that happen within the debating chamber below. But the glass and steel cupola creates problems with solar gain; the transparent skin allows heat from the sun to penetrate into and thus to overheat the space. The obvious solution (using a covering of screens or louvres) would compromise the view across the city.

Foster + Partners counter the problem in two ways; firstly the glass panels of the cupola overlap each other and have a ventilation gap between them to allow air to flow through the space. Cool air enters the debating chamber at its base and as it heats up it rises and escapes, thus encouraging more cool air to enter (stack effect). Secondly, the architects developed a large moveable screen that is attached to the edge of the ramp and tracks the path of the sun around the dome. It shades the debating chamber from the direct heat and light of the sun without compromising the view and the symbolic power of the remodelling. The problems created by the dome are thus solved in a sympathetic and passive manner.

Introduction > **Climate** > Light

'Occupants report high levels of satisfaction with their workspace when there are large amounts of daylight.'

**Mary Ann Lazarus
Sandra Mandler
William Odell**

Climate: Focus study 2

**Top:
The gathering space**
Natural foliage animates the foyer.

**Above:
Mechanical services**
Heat is extracted from the space through an artificial air extraction system.

**Facing page:
Interior of the foyer**
Natural light floods into the space.

Name:
The Palace of Music

Location:
Valencia, Spain

Date:
1987

Designer:
José María de Paredes

Throughout history, a number of methods to control the effect of the environment, and temperature in particular, on the interior have been employed by architects and designers.

The Palacio de la Musica is situated in the old dry river bed of the Turia, which runs through the centre of Valencia. The concert hall was constructed in 1987 and was one of the first of a series of cultural buildings and gardens intended to connect the centre of the city with the sea.

The 'river garden' concept was for a long public park that contained a progression of walks, water features and shading plants and trees. Santiago Calatrava has created the majority of these features, but it was the experienced auditorium designer, José María de Paredes (architect for the concert halls in Madrid and Granada) who designed this building.

The building is very regular and simple; it is a huge white block with a large curved glass enclosure attached to it. While the solid back is integrated into the tight urban context, the glazed vault has a direct relationship with the water gardens within the river bed. This stretch of fountains and pools was designed by Ricardo Bofill and is an expression of his oversized and classically inspired language. The inside of the transparent hall has the appearance of a greenhouse, with steamy foliage and a warm atmosphere.

Direct summer sunlight is excluded from the building by the overhanging canopy but the welcome winter sun is allowed to penetrate into the heart of the building. The glazed vault heats the space; it acts as an enormous conservatory, while natural ventilation encourages air movement.

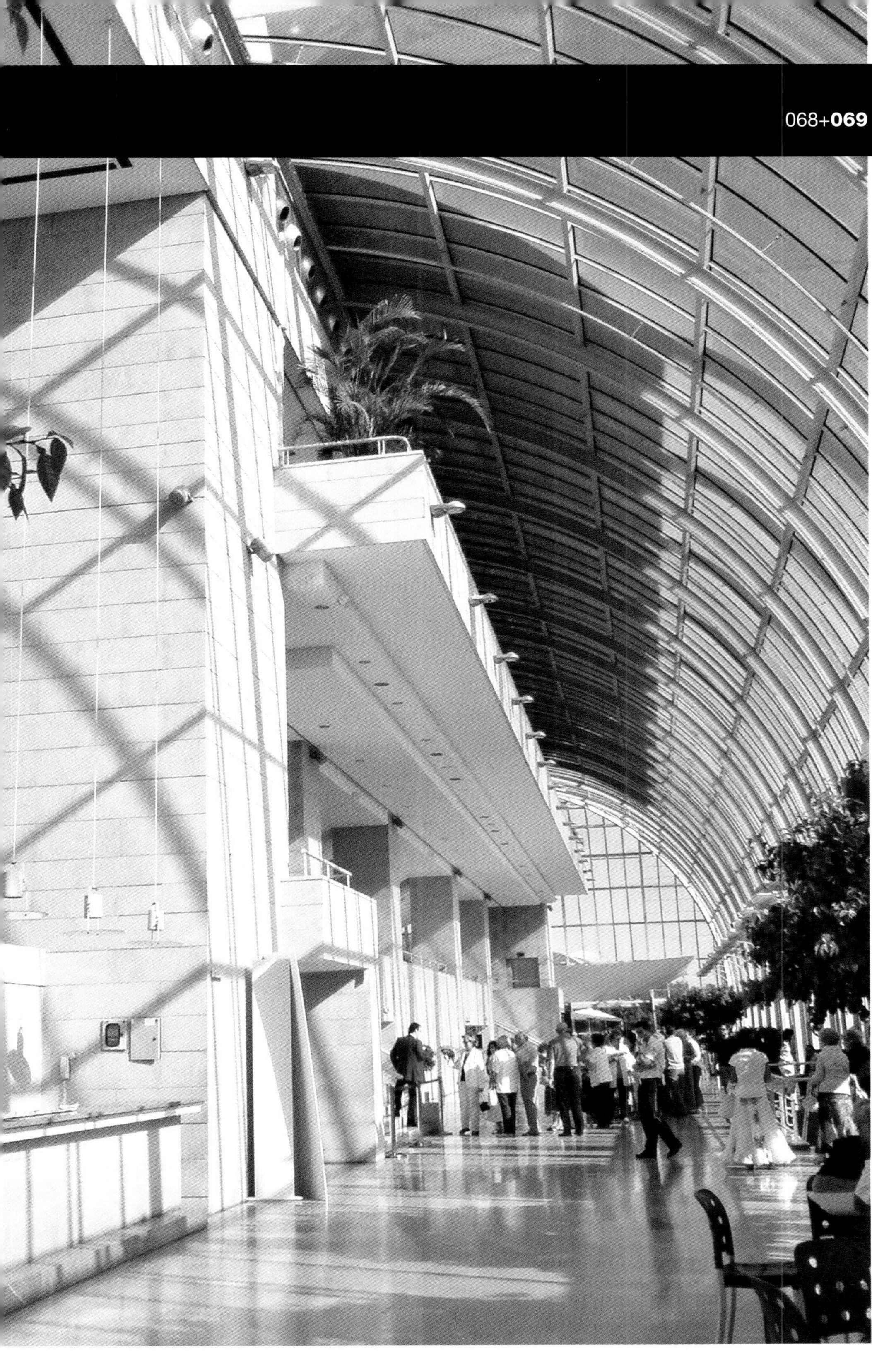

Light is the most fundamental of all materials; without it form cannot be visualised, space cannot be appreciated and atmosphere cannot be created. Light can control: it can direct, movement can be suggested, objects and places can be illuminated and accentuated and it can be used to change perceptions, both subtly and more dramatically.

Light: Focus study 1

Name:
Bregenz Art Gallery

Location:
Bregenz, Austria

Date:
1997

Designer:
Peter Zumthor

The architect can use elements of the design to control how and when light is admitted into the interior.

The Bregenz Art Gallery stands on the edge of Lake Constance, an enigmatic and iconic building in among a collection of unusual and stylistically diverse architecture. The museum exists in two parts: a short matt black box that encloses the service areas, such as the café, shop and offices; and a high, illuminated structure that contains the galleries. This tall steel-framed edifice is clad in large, overlapping opaque glass panels, thus giving the impression of a skin of glazed scales. During the day the building reflects light from the lake and the sky, but at night the artificial glow of the lights within the galleries bursts from the interior and illuminates the façade.

The enigmatic and brooding quality of the museum is reinforced by the insular focus; there are no views of the dramatic landscape from within the galleries, the visitor is required to focus only on the art and not the location. But the irregular presence of natural light is always apparent; it is dispersed through the gallery spaces by an ingenious distribution system that catches the light and then spreads it across the depth of the gallery rooms. Each level is double height but a glass ceiling splits the volume horizontally. Concrete walls contain the lower half and provide hanging space for the works of art. The top half is free from massive divisions, thus allowing the light to filter across the width of the space and be reflected into the galleries. None of this is apparent from the exterior during the day as it is discreetly hidden by the unrelenting obscurity of the glazed façade, but at night and when artificially illuminated, the layers of the interior 'stack' of floors are exposed.

The absorption and storage capacity of the unclad concrete allows the climate of the galleries to remain relatively stable, obviating the need for the clutter of service pipes and air movement systems. The suspended glass ceiling obscures the back-up systems of wiring and artificial light that automatically kicks in when the natural light dips below requirements. All in all the galleries are stripped clear of the clutter and detritus of electrics and plumbing, and are focussed, contemplative spaces for the observation of modern art.

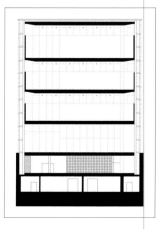

Environment and the interior

Facing page:
The glazed façade
of the gallery
The building is clad in a uniform
layer of overlapping glass panels.

Below:
Gallery interior
Natural light is dissipated through
the false ceiling space and
into the depths of the gallery.

'The spatial constellation of the slabs varies
the orientation of the light, generates shadows
and reflections. It tempers the mood of the
light and gives depth to the room. The constantly
fluctuating light gives the impression that the
building is breathing.'

Peter Zumthor

Right:
Foyer
The supporting structure
shields the spaces from the
effects of direct natural light.

Facing page:
Section
Each floor is treated as an
independent tray, supported
within the envelope of the
building. Note the gaps, which
allow natural light into the
false ceilings.

Climate > **Light** > Temperature

Right:
Aerial view of building
The bi-part of the building is clearly visible. The ONL seawater pavilion overhangs the beach while the NOX freshwater pavilion is on land.

Light: Focus study 2

Name:
H2O Expo, saltwater pavilion

Location:
Neeltje Jans, The Netherlands

Date:
1997

Designer:
ONL

Artificial light can be manipulated by the designer to provoke a reaction from the visitor. This process might be a continuation of the exterior conditions, or in stark contrast to them.

The Dutch have always had an intimate relationship with water and this project, a hydro-pavilion, effectively exploits this connection. ONL and NOX were commissioned to design this joint and strangely hybrid building that exhibits educational material about Dutch technical advances in water engineering. ONL designed the saltwater pavilion on the sea side, while NOX designed the freshwater pavilion on the land side.

Sophisticated computer modelling has taken an increasingly important role in controlling and shaping real environments. In this project software and programming has not only produced the form of the building but it also controls the experience within it. This is achieved by the assimilation of environmental data taken from marine scanners and radars, and combining this information with visitor recognising sensors, in order to create an unusual interior experience.

The exterior of the seawater pavilion has evolved via computer drawing and manipulation to resemble an organism, looking like something between a beached whale and a stealth bomber. It soars for 12 metres across a pebbly beach, sliding towards the waters of the Oosterschelde and hovering above the water's edge.

The black, menacing exterior contrasts strongly with the interior, which is very much a virtual environment. It is illuminated with complicated graphics, while electronic sensors trigger information and lights. The interior of the pavilion is linked to a weather station that constantly feeds environmental data such as wind speeds, water levels and other climatic information to the 'onboard' computers. The system then translates this data and calculates emotive responses based on the number of visitors passing through the pavilion. The raw data is converted to midi-impulses that trigger sound and light and consequently mix the real-time experience of the environment with the virtual responses of the visitor. Fibre optic lightscapes, film projections and sound emanate from the polycarbonate-lined interior. This is intended to simulate the fluid form of the pavilion and the surrounding contextual climatic conditions. The exhibition is an abstracted representation of the environmental conditions that surround the pavilion. The visitor travels through the interior and experiences the climatic conditions of the delta, thus blurring the boundaries between real and virtual environments.

Environment and the interior

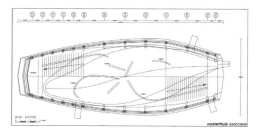

plan wetlab

oosterhuis associates

Facing page:
Plan
The sensuous curves of the
pavilion interior form the
exhibition elements of the space.

Top:
Pavilion interior
The intensity of the light is
dictated by the weather
and the attitude of the visitor.

Above:
Exhibition gallery
The ever-changing light
within the space has
a disorientating effect.

Climate > **Light** > Temperature

We build houses to keep a number of variables within our immediate environment at a constant level. We can only live comfortably in a fairly narrow band of temperature differences. The modern method of temperature control is through air conditioning, but a number of more passive systems have evolved and are increasingly becoming viable once again.

Above:
The garden
Movement encourages water vapour to enter the atmosphere and cool the environment.

Left:
The red castle
The palace occupies a strategic hilltop position.

Facing page:
Interior of the palace
Channels of water cool the rooms of the palace.

Environment and the interior

'When [the court] is provided with greenery and water, and is shaded, it acts as a cooling well and actually modifies the micro-climate by lowering the ground temperature.'
Amos Rapoport

Temperature: Focus study 1

Name:
The Alhambra (The Red Palace)

Location:
Granada, Spain

Date:
Eighth and ninth centuries
(exact date unknown)

Designer:
Unknown

Passive methods of temperature control are becoming viable alternatives to air conditioning. Many of these methods are based upon processes that have evolved over many hundreds of years.

The Alhambra, from the Arabic *al-Qalat al-Hamra* – the red castle, is a medieval Moorish fortress occupying a hilly terrace on the edge of the city of Granada in Spain. It was the walled residence of Muslim kings throughout the thirteenth, fourteenth and fifteenth centuries (it is thought that the complex was originally built in the eighth or ninth century as a military area). Thirteen towers flank this exquisite palace, which has, in the centuries of its existence, evolved into a fine collection of carefully ordered buildings, rooms, gardens and landscapes. The Alhambra has gradually developed to accommodate six palaces, numerous bath houses and spaces linked by gardens that are watered by a sophisticated irrigation system.

The climate in southern Spain for much of the year is hot and at the height of summer it can become unbearable. The Moors designed a simple method of cooling the spaces within the Alhambra, exploiting the small amount of air movement and water. Water continually runs through the palaces in carefully designed shallow pools, streams and channels. Some of these are quite large, such as those found in the *Generalife*, or leisure villa of the sultans, but others are much more modest – often little more than a small bubbling fountain feeding a small channel. A slight breeze is created through the use of the stack effect; warm air rises at the centre of the courtyards, thus encouraging cooler air from shaded rooms to replace it. This is dragged through small openings in the walls, inducing a degree of speed, which generates a gentle wind that passes through the adjoining rooms. The important reaction is the water movement combined with the passage of air through the space. This encourages evaporation and the water vapour to cool the space. The palaces are cooled in a delicate and seductive manner.

Light > **Temperature** > Orientation

Above:
Exterior of the domes
The building nestles within
a disused clay pit.

Left:
The wall of the biome
A rigid hexagonal structure
supports the triple layer
of ETFE foil.

Nick Grimshaw

Nick Grimshaw is an architect with a passion for
engineering. His early buildings were distinctly 'high-tech',
often using overtly industrial design language. His
practice has a reputation for rational yet creative buildings
and they describe their approach as, 'structure, space,
skin'. Their international portfolio includes Waterloo
Terminal, UK; Ijburg Bridge, The Netherlands; Ludwig
Erhard Haas, Berlin and the Southern Cross Station
in Melbourne, Australia.

Environment and the interior

Temperature: Focus study 2

Name:
Eden Project

Location:
Cornwall, England

Date:
2001

Designer:
Grimshaw Architects

The use and control of warmth from the sun has been a common method of heating a space for thousands of years. The invention of glass meant that spaces could also be protected from the wind, thus enabling better retention of the accumulated heat. A widespread method of retaining solar gain within domestic properties is the conservatory. This works on the same principles as the greenhouse, by encouraging sunlight to enter a space while discouraging the cooling effects of the wind. The long rays of the winter sun are very welcome during cold months and these can be exploited as a passive method of providing heat to a much larger area. Air heated within the enclosed space can then be encouraged to infiltrate the whole house.

In the past, exotic fruits such as oranges, peaches and lemons were grown in orangeries – garden buildings with large windows on the south side. These orangeries tended to be found in prosperous gardens throughout the Renaissance and up until the nineteenth century. These were natural precursors of the greenhouse – a small, fully glazed building, used particularly for the cultivation of plants. They are quite common in residential gardens but much larger examples are found in public gardens, such as those at Kew in the UK. The greenhouse provides a controlled climate much warmer than natural or local conditions.

The Eden Project in Cornwall in the UK utilises the controlled heat from sun to create an atmosphere that is far warmer than the UK's natural climate. It is a collection of transparent 'biomes' that provide a controlled environment to encourage a rich diversity of plant growth.

The biomes are constructed from a galvanised tubular steel frame, which is then clad with a triple layer of hexagonal panels of ETFE foil (Ethylene Tetrafluoroethylene). ETFE is a transparent, recyclable foil that is very strong, transparent to UV light and is not degraded by sunlight. The covered biomes are incredibly well insulated to conserve heat and, therefore, energy. The three layers of ETFE foil within the hexagons are blown apart by air forming an insulating pillow. The climate is controlled using sophisticated computerised systems for automatic ventilation and heating. The solid back wall absorbs heat during the day and releases it at night. The plants themselves also help to control the climate; when it gets hotter they give off more water, which cools the air.

The Eden Project could be described as a modern incarnation of the orangery, a structure dating back hundreds of years that utilises and retains the heat from the sun and protects from the wind and rain, thus altering, within a very small space, the prevailing climate.

Right:
Exotic foliage
The temperature-controlled microclimate allows non-indigenous plants to thrive.

Orientation is the determination of the relative physical position of something in relation to something else. A building or interior can be positioned in such a way that it either takes advantage of, or shies away from, a particular physical feature or condition. This might, for example, be the sun or the wind; the principal rooms in a building may be constructed to take advantage of the afternoon sun; or the terrace may be positioned away from the prevailing wind. It may be a physical feature such as a neighbouring building that could potentially overlook the space or it may be things further away, such as geographical features. The designer can employ a number of methods to control the orientation of a space.

Top:
The building in context
The three connecting boxes are a representation of the three hills.

Above:
Room 1
The brutal interior spaces are linked with simple openings.

Left:
Room 2
The raw, simple galleries are top-lit.

Facing page:
Section
The three crude boxes of the gallery are top-lit and naturally ventilated.

'The architect brings order to the world through building. The artistic and scientific tools of the architect or designer are brought into contact with the site and architecture emerges through a process of negotiation with physical context and lived experience.'
Dominic Roberts

Orientation: Focus study 1

Name:
La Congiunta

Location:
Giornico, Switzerland

Date:
1992

Designer:
Peter Märkli and Stefan Bellwader

An awareness of the interesting connections between the interior and its physical environment can be heightened through the orientation of an interior space.

La Congiunta (the marriage) is a small gallery hidden away in the bottom of the Leventina valley in Switzerland. It is not a museum in the conventional sense, there is no welcome at the front door nor bookshop or café. Instead, the visitor has to pick up a key from the bar in the nearest village to get into the space. The building is little more than three raw boxes, and is reminiscent of a bunker with cold, fair-faced concrete walls, and a harsh, austere atmosphere. The entrance is a steel door, accessed from a raised steel footplate, and once the door is opened the interior is equally brutal – a raw concrete space, cool and still. The space is naturally top-lit, sunlight washes the grey walls of the gallery through the steel roof lantern.

The building is orientated in relation to the valley and the road by which it is accessed. It abstracts the surrounding landscape by synthesising the three hills of the valley to provide the formal gesture of the three connected boxes of the building. The uncompromising language and aesthetic of the space is a fitting response to the rugged landscape in which it is positioned and the tough, elegant sculptures that it has been built to house. The building is an unusual union between this landscape and the sculptures of Hans Josephsohn, a local artist who creates robust uncompromising sculptures from poured concrete and stone. The three stepped, windowless blocks reflect the surrounding hills and separate the interior into three gallery spaces, each representing a phase of the sculptor's work. There are none of the usual comforts associated with galleries; no lighting, heating or floor coverings, only the bare essentials of the materials of the construction. The language of the building, the sculptures and the landscape are fused together in one elegant space.

Temperature > **Orientation** > View/aspect

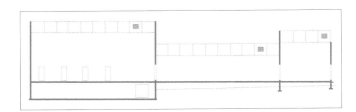

Orientation: Focus study 2

Name:
Summer Hill

Location:
Cumbria, England

Date:
2006

Designer:
Francis Roberts Architects

Spaces can be positioned so that although they are adjacent, they are oriented in opposite directions, thus creating a psychological detachment.

Summer Hill is an apt name for this well proportioned Georgian House. It is situated in a sheltered yet sunny position in the south of the Lake District, north-west England, with views of the hills; from the mountains to the North, across sumptuous farmland, to Morecambe Bay in the South. Francis Roberts Architects have designed a sensitive and complete extension to this building. The new element is a complete home and although it is joined to the original building, it is designed to be absolutely separate from it. The architects have created an addition that does not compromise the original, while acting as a complete and whole house in its own right.

The approach that the architects took was to extend the building at the rear, thus retaining the magnificent classical façade. The old faces in one direction; a controlled and picturesque vista towards the entrance of the grounds, while the new relates to the previously hidden hilly farmland. The entrance and the windows of the extension are deliberately positioned so that they do not overlook or interfere with the Georgian building. The language and technology of the addition is obviously derived from the context, but is also very much part of the twenty-first century.

The architects have successfully created a modern extension to an existing building that is orientated in exactly the opposite direction to the original structure without compromising the integrity of either.

Top:
The terrace
The extension is orientated and integrated with the landscape.

Above:
View from the bedroom
The interior has a direct relationship with the landscape.

Facing page:
Building in the landscape
The original building is on the left and the extension is on the right.

Orientation

'Orientation' literally means the determination of the position of something or someone in relation to something or somebody else. What is important is the relationship that is established between the two. This may be as simple as a compass point. The word 'orient' is thought to be derived from *oriens*, meaning East. In the Middle Ages many maps were drawn with East at the top but today it is most common for North to be at the top.

A building or interior can respond directly to a particular physical feature. It may be positioned to take advantage of a specific view or it may be designed as a retort or counterpoint to a precise object or element. The view may be framed and only appreciated from a fixed point within the interior or the whole building may be orientated as a reaction to an activity or function.

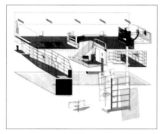

Top:
Exploded isometric drawing
The building is constructed from a kit of beautifully designed elements.

Above:
Photomontage of the project
The building is buried deep into the urban context.

View/aspect: Focus study 1

Name:
Blackburn House

Location:
London, England

Date:
1988

Designer:
Bolles + Wilson

Within an uncompromising and crowded urban environment, the designer can create long views through the interior of a building, while carefully controlling any exterior outlook.

The architects Bolles + Wilson were commissioned by Janice and David Blackburn to remodel the top two floors of a Hampstead mews house, in order to accommodate both themselves and their collection of contemporary art. The immediate dense context of the building meant that neighbouring buildings compromised any sight lines or views from the interior of the house, a feature that fostered an introverted approach to the interior design. The requirement for the top floors of the building to act as a gallery necessitated the designers to create large amounts of uninterrupted wall space.

In response to all this, the views within the house have been carefully controlled. A huge double-height entrance space is animated by light from a tall, inclined bay window that asymmetrically juts out of the rectangular house. The full height of the window is decorated and obscured with sandblasted glass, allowing light to enter the interior but eclipsing the view to the all-too-close neighbours. Small areas of untreated glass give the indistinct impression of movement and activity. The only space that affords a clear view of the outside is the study. This narrow, bottle-shaped room is lined with timber and comes to a point directly opposite the desk. The perspective of the room is accentuated and the view is channelled by the long thin point of the space towards the view – a tree outside the room.

Environment and the interior

Above:
The plywood-lined study
The room is focussed on the tree
directly outside the window.

Right:
The first floor plan
The interior is very tightly planned.
Note the funnel-shaped study on
the left-hand side.

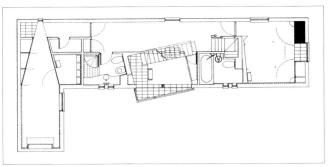

Orientation > **View/aspect** > Materials

View/aspect: Focus study 2

Name:
Dundee Contemporary
Arts Centre (DCA)

Location:
Dundee, Scotland

Date:
1999

Designer:
Richard Murphy Architects

The designer can create views through the three-dimensional interior space of a building.

The Dundee Contemporary Arts Centre was formed from the reworking of a large derelict brick warehouse, once a favourite haunt of Dundee's skateboarders. The building occupies an awkward site between the city and the river Tay, hemmed in by the cathedral and an elaborate nineteenth-century villa. To complicate things further there is an eight-metre slope across the site and 24-hour public right of way is required from the city centre to the river. Into this compact site Murphy has inserted arts facilities, galleries, cinemas, workshops, support spaces such as a café/bar and shop, plus offices for the gallery and Dundee City Council.

The careful reworking of the warehouse caused the building to be cut open to accommodate the new spaces and functions. The awkward yet prominent site prompted Murphy to organise the interior using an L-shaped plan. This allows the main public spaces to be distributed along an internal three-storey 'street'. Rather than enter the more obvious river side of the building, the entrance faces Dundee and connects the building to the city, using the river as a backdrop to the open views through the interior. The busy internal street allows these direct, sun-filled views across the building. The visitor standing in the cantilevered window can overlook 'the street' and view, as well as be viewed, by the throng below. Cinema goers are unaware as they cross the car park in front of the river that they are framed by the open screen shutter, an element that will then close to accept the projection of the film. Even drinkers in the bar can catch a skewed glimpse of the inside of the cinema as a film is showing. This extrovert building is a people-watcher's paradise, maximising the stunning landscape into which it is neatly orientated to get the best views of Dundee and its inhabitants.

Top:
The warehouse before conversion
The building has a relationship with the sea.

Above:
Axonometric
The building is enlarged and opened up on the city side.

Facing page top:
Entrance
Artificial light floods from the building and advertises the new use.

Facing page:
The internal street
The circulation through the building reconnects the city with the sea.

Environment and the interior

'It is almost entirely through vision that the environment is apprehended.'
Gordon Cullen

The materials used within an interior have an intrinsic relationship between the space itself and the environmental conditions that surround it. They allow the designer to create a new physical feel to the space – this might be a continuation of, or reaction to, the surrounding elements. Choice of materials can alter the effect of acoustics, temperature, and light as well as the relationship between the interior and its context.

Above:
Interior
The furniture arrangement within the space reflects its simple nature. Note the recovered altarpiece set within the top-lit alcove.

Top right:
The chapel
The simplicity of the building is apparent from the street entrance.

Right:
Between the walls
The circulation space between the inner and outer walls is particularly atmospheric.

Below right:
The chapel wall
The rammed-earth construction contains fragments of the original church.

Materials: Focus study 1

Name:
The Church of Reconciliation

Location:
Berlin, Germany

Date:
2000

Designer:
Rudolf Reitermann and
Peter Sassenroth

Creating visual and aural
effects though the use of specific
materials can reinforce the
connection between a building
and its context and environment.

The Church of Reconciliation
occupies a particularly poignant
position in German history and
geography. When the dividing
wall between East and West
Berlin was constructed, the
patch of land on which the new
church now stands was left in
'no-man's-land'. It was actually
just on the eastern side of the
wall, but was inaccessible.
The original neo-Gothic church,
which was opened in 1895, was
demolished in 1985 because
it was deemed to restrict the
guards' sightlines. After German
reunification a competition was
organised to reclaim the site
and construct a new Church of
Reconciliation, a symbol of hope
and friendship. The foundations
of the original church still existed
and many meaningful objects
such as the baptismal font,
communion vessels, the altar
itself and even the church bells
were returned from safe keeping.

The architects, Reitermann and
Sassenroth, designed the chapel
to sit on top of the old ruined
altar space. In plan the chapel
is made of two concentric oval
shapes; an outer rain-screen ring
constructed from timber slats
forms a semi-open circulation
space and an inner top-lit oval
room enclosed by walls of
rammed earth forms the space
for worship. Brick rubble from
the historic structure was blended
with the rammed earth mixture
as a symbol of remembrance
and the walls glisten with pieces
of rock and stone compacted
into its layers. The rammed earth
floor, treated with natural wax,
expresses the connection to the
soil. The wall controls the climate
of the space by enclosing the
chapel and protecting it from
the outside as well as offering
a connection to the history of the
site. The bells of the old church
are now housed in a timber
carillon placed at the Bernauer
Strasse entrance to the chapel
and ring at the call for worship.
The original altar piece was
re-hung and, most significantly,
the foundations of the old
church are exposed through
a glass plate in the floor. The
congregation is continually
reminded of the past, of the
history and the context of this
extraordinary church.

Below:
Plan
The rammed-earth circular
walls are surrounded by the
timber rain screen.

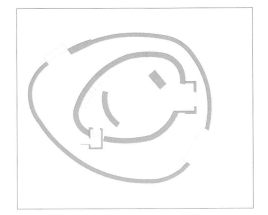

Materials: Focus study 2

Name:
Irish Film Centre

Location:
Temple Bar, Dublin, Ireland

Date:
1992

Designer:
O'Donnell + Tuomey

The designer can use materials to reveal layers of the building and its surrounding environment's history.

Temple Bar, a dense urban area in the centre of Dublin, has suffered severe neglect from a lack of investment and depopulation. This is due in some part to the area being earmarked for mass-demolition in order to make way for a massive traffic terminal. When this idea was abandoned, the council organised a competition to regenerate the area. The council was determined to take a contextual approach – it was only too aware of the destructive nature of post-war developments in the city. The area alongside the river Liffey occupies a prominent site in the heart of the city. Group 91, a team of local architects and designers, proposed a sensitive reworking of the area, based on the introduction of key public cultural buildings. These would generate interest and activity in the area – other activities, such as cafés and small shops would then follow.

O'Donnell and Tuomey, who were part of this group, were also commissioned to design the Irish Film Centre. The Quaker Meeting House, positioned on the edge of a major public space within the regeneration project, Meeting House Square, was the chosen site for this. This assemblage consisted of nine different buildings, all distributed around what was once a quiet, open courtyard. The church had no discernible front façade as a result of an old by-law that forbade non-established churches from having a prominent street presence. The collection of buildings was large enough to house two cinemas, a café, ticket offices, a bookshop and ancillary spaces, such as offices and storage.

The cinemas could only have been positioned in the sufficiently substantial main meeting room and the smaller ladies' room. This quickly established the main elements and the shared projector room. The rest of the functions were distributed around the newly enclosed courtyard. This courtyard acts as the public face of the cinema – the IFC still has no prominent street frontage so access is through small, discreet alleys and arcades. The courtyard is the key element within the design, around which all of the activities are distributed. Although it is covered and is a totally inside space, it is designed with a deliberately outdoor character. The folded, glazed roof admits substantial amounts of natural light, reinforcing the exterior feeling. The floor, walls and signage are also designed with a robust outdoor quality. The floor is made of limestone flags inlaid with concentric steel circles; these serve to identify the centre of the space. The old exterior brick walls of the meeting house are now the interior walls of the Irish Film Centre.

All the materials are a mixture of 'found' surfaces and newly imposed exterior quality elements. The revealing layers of history of the buildings were exposed through the different surface characteristics of the site. The designers then applied their own contemporary layer of meaning.

Left:
Courtyard roof
The folded glazed roof reinforces the exterior quality of the space.

Below left:
Site plan
The film centre at the bottom of the picture is contained within its context.

Below:
Interior of the courtyard
The new wall butts up against the original building.

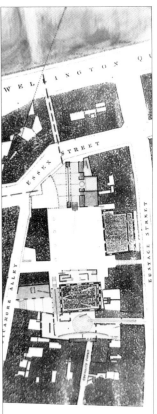

O'Donnell + Tuomey

O'Donnell + Tuomey are well known for their sensitive and contextual approach to design. The practice regards the investigation and uncovering of the characteristics and qualities of the site as an integral part of the design process. They modestly regard their contribution to architecture as a twenty-first-century layer of archaeology.

View/aspect > **Materials**

**The reuse of an existing building
not only provides a link to our cultural
heritage and collective memory;
it is also an environmentally friendly
act. The amount of resources needed
for reuse is far less than those
necessary for new-build. Efficient
responses to resources, weather and
recycling can also provide significant
benefits to such strategies.**

Name:
Water Tower (see pp 116+117)

Location:
Shooters Hill, London, England

Date:
2000

Designer:
Loates-Taylor Shannon Ltd
(LTS Architects)

Environmental awareness

To reuse a building is probably one of the most sustainable methods that a designer can employ. After all, the structure already exists and a lot of the services are already in place; the embodied energy in these elements is saved. Reusing a structure also reduces the amount of new resources necessary to construct a building.

Resources

This attitude can also inform the nature of the remodelling: the designer can use local materials, thus saving the energy embodied in transportation; natural, non-toxic materials can be specified and, if possible, the building can be powered by renewable energy resources such as wind or solar power.

Weather

Another sustainable act is to design a building or interior so that it can be used in an environmentally friendly manner. This includes making use of natural light and ventilation. Light can be thrown into the depths of spaces; this will save on artificial light and will also provide the occupant with a connection with the outside. The intensity of natural light fluctuates depending upon the time of day and the season of the year. Trapping the heat from solar gain will save on heating costs and cross-breeze ventilation is a natural way of cooling a space.

Recycling

Local buildings or rather those constructed in the vernacular tradition will often already embody a number of environmentally friendly and sustainable features. These buildings have evolved in a direct relationship with their immediate context and, as such, have developed methods of controlling their habitat and particular climatic conditions. Discovering and re-discovering methods of reducing energy use are one of the twenty-first century's foremost preoccupations, and the attitude taken by the designer can contribute to this debate.

Found object

The use and reuse of found objects can create links with society's collective memory. A whole object can be placed in an unnatural situation, accentuating the qualities of the object itself and the new space that it occupies.

Occupation

The designer can create spaces that encourage the user to employ sustainable and energy-efficient methods of living and working. If the designer is aware of the methods of naturally controlling the environmental conditions within an interior, a space that is both comfortable and sustainable can be created.

Above:

TBWA\Hakuhodo offices,
Tokyo, Japan (see pp 108+109).

The reuse of existing buildings is one the most sustainable approaches to architectural design. The designer can adopt a methodology that is not only sensitive to sustainable issues within the design of the interior, but can also provide an interior that has a sustainable attitude to the method in which it is occupied.

Environmental awareness: Focus study 1

Name:
Coal House

Location:
Kishorn, Scotland

Date:
1998

Designer:
Unknown

Buildings with an unusual history or function that has become obsolete can be reused with surprising and delightful results.

This house has responded to its context in a number of ways. Firstly it is an existing building; it was once the village coal store. The fuel was brought by boat to the shore where it was offloaded on to the next-door jetty and stored. The building is conveniently central to the village and is easily accessible by boat, although until relatively recently the village itself was difficult to access by road.

The materials used in the restoration and remodelling are local and sympathetic to the environment. The house is constructed from the same colours as the rocks that it sits on and the roof is as black as the angry sky on a stormy day. The language is also appropriate to the huge dramatic landscape in which it is situated.

The internal organisation also reflects the unusual context; the main living rooms are situated on the upper floor, thus taking advantage of the incredible views across Loch Kishorn to the mountains of Skye. Long horizontal windows at first-floor level reinforce the orthogonal quality of the building while the small windows at ground-floor level reflect the need for protection against the weather and the sea. The remodelled building is a sympathetic and appropriate response to its environment.

Above:
Entrance to the house
Tremendous views are provided through the long strip window from the first-floor living room.

Facing page:
The house in context
The home perches precariously at the water's edge, within the dramatic landscape.

'Were thoughts like these the Dream of ancient Time?
Peculiar only to some Age, or Clime?
And does not Nature thoughts like these impart,
Breathe in the Soul, and write upon the Heart?'

John Langhorne

Sustainability and the existing interior

Above:
Internal courtyard
The modernist curved balconies reinforce the light and airy quality within the internal courtyard.

Left:
Circulation in the new space
Light is admitted into this internal space through the north-facing glazed wall and the south-facing roof light.

Facing page top:
View through the external courtyard
The extension completes the original building in a light and modern manner.

Facing page bottom:
Plan
The new addition completes the old building.

'(Asplund) was a leader in the moderation of the Modernist vocabulary towards a greater continuity with architectural traditions.'

Claes Caldenby
Jöran Lindvall
Wilfred Wang

Environmental awareness: Focus study 2

Name:
Gothenburg Law Courts

Location:
Gothenburg, Sweden

Date:
1934–37

Designer:
Erik Gunnar Asplund

An extension to a building can establish a direct relationship between the new and old. This is often most obvious on the façade.

Asplund's addition to the Gothenburg Law Courts is a respectful and courteous engagement with the original. The front of the building shows how the modern has augmented the classical in a sympathetic yet responsive manner.

However, within the interior, Asplund was much more assertive. The original semi-enclosed courtyard was completed and a new internal courtyard or atrium-type space created. Thus, two contrasting open spaces were formed; one inside and the other outside. A fully glazed wall and the major vertical circulation routes separate these. The new is uncompromisingly modern and clearly Scandinavian. The interior courtyard is clad with sensuous curves of glowing pine. These are illuminated by the natural light that pours into the new triple-height atrium space; constant northerly light from the glazed wall and warmer southerly light from the roof. Although the sense of movement and promenade is very strong within the building, its dignity has not been compromised.

The stairs have a processional quality; the heights of the risers have been reduced and the length of the treads increased, thus imbuing the space with a ceremonial air. The interior is awash with light and air, it conveys the modernist ideal of promoting health through contact with the natural fresh environment. All of Asplund's work is drawn from the Scandinavian vernacular, combined with a complete understanding of modernist principles.

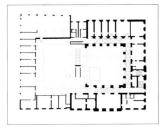

Designers have the opportunity to act in a sustainable and environmentally friendly manner when specifying the materials to be used within the remodelling of an existing building. There are a number of factors to be considered, including the proximity of the materials to the site – transportation of materials consumes huge amounts of energy. Using local resources is also likely to result in an interior that responds to climatic conditions effectively and can create strong ties with the building's context and history.

Resources: Focus study 1

Name:
The Archbishopric Museum

Location:
Hamar, Norway

Date:
1967–79

Designer:
Sverre Fehn

The materials used in a new design and the elements that connect them can reflect those used in the original.

The Archbishopric Museum, sometimes known as the Hedmark Cathedral Museum, is situated in the small Norwegian Town of Hamar, just north of Oslo. The museum was designed to disclose the strata of time by exposing the various layers of history within the remains of a medieval fortress. The buildings were used as a farmstead from the sixteenth century, but had been allowed to decay. This collection of ruins (including the remnants of the cathedral and bishop's priory) on an important medieval route has been rebuilt/completed using modern building techniques.

There is no doubt about the difference between the old and new, no attempt has been made to integrate the two, they simply co-exist.

The barn is U-shaped and sits across the ruins of the fortress, incorporating some of the ruined walls into its own construction. The barn is rural in its construction and use of materials. Fehn has retained the stone construction of the walls and has simply enclosed the existing. The new roof of the barn is constructed from tiles and is supported by a robust timber frame that is positioned either on or inside the thick stone walls, depending on the structural integrity of the remains. The buildings are penetrated by a concrete structure of ramps, platforms, balconies and rooms. This forms an elevated route giving the viewer an overview of revealed layers below and access to discreetly placed top-lit cells containing small historical artefacts.

The materials used within the project reflect the contextual position of the settlement in many ways. They have a purity that parallels the qualities of the original. The concrete, wood and roof tiles are raw, unadorned and natural. The methods of attaching materials together also have a rawness; the huge and minimal glass sheets covering the openings are simply bolted to the walls and the exposed steel fastenings connecting the timber roof structure together are crude and unadorned. The materials used and the manner in which they are put together reflects the hard and uncompromising climate in which the buildings are situated. Sverre Fehn's interventions respond to the nature of the site, creating a twentieth-century museum that is as much part of the landscape as the original buildings were.

Sustainability and the existing interior

Facing page:
Glazed opening
The glass is crudely bolted to
the exterior of the building.
It offers little thermal protection.

'As at Scarpa's Castelvecchio the architect benefits
from the discipline imposed by the interpretation of the
archaeology and the existing structures.'

Dominic Roberts

Top:
The bridge
Natural light enters the space
through the broken wall.

Above:
Materials
The concrete is as brutal as the
crude stone building. Note the
laminated timber roof structure
above the concrete walkway.

Left:
Museum interior
The concrete ramp hovers
above the archaeological remains.
The space is top-lit by glazed
openings in the roof.

Environmental awareness > **Resources** > Weather

Resources: Focus study 2

Name:
West End Refurbishment
Programme

Location:
Morecambe, England

Date:
2005

Designer:
Arca

A single material can tie a number of disparate parts or spaces together; it can provide the link that connects together what may otherwise appear to be a random collection of elements.

This is the approach that Arca took to the refurbishment of a series of large Victorian terraced houses in a run-down area of Morecambe, a seaside town in the north-west of England. Timber was used to unite the revitalised dwellings. The architects prepared a sort of 'pattern book' of different features that could be attached to the buildings, such as bay windows, dormer windows or porches. They were all made of timber and designed to be distinct, but obviously part of a family of features. About twenty properties scattered across the area were refurbished using this new contemporary kit of architectural parts technique. The dwellings were provided with new external features, such as balconies, decking and boundary fences all in timber, with some properties given whole extensions in wood.

Internally, the boundaries of the rooms were lined with timber to achieve modern insulation standards and new wooden windows articulated a sense of the interior lining emerging on to the street. In this way the relationship between inside and outside became slightly blurred, the actual transition point between the two uncertain, thus allowing the balcony, exterior terrace or decked area to be used quite casually as part of the living space.

The distinctive new additions are an obvious sign of improvement that link a collection of individual properties in a modest yet distinctive manner.

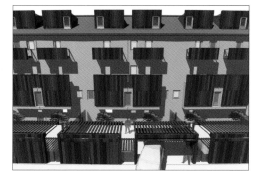

Left:
Elevations
The simple timber elements reinvigorate the façades of the houses.

Facing page:
Long elevation
The timber elements tie a series
of disparate properties together.

Below:
Wooden balconies
The timber balconies add
an essential sense of warmth
to the properties.

'Again and again there is the sensuality of the material –
how it feels, what it looks like: does it look dull, does
it shimmer and sparkle? Its smell. Is it hard or soft,
flexible, cold or warm, smooth or rough? What colour
is it and which colours does it reveal on its surface?'

Andrea Deplazes

The extent to which the designer can control and make use of the prevailing weather conditions can have a significant impact on the sustainability and energy efficiency of an existing interior. The architect or designer must be aware of specific weather conditions and must create methods to deal with them effectively. For instance, despite the moderate climate in the UK, there are striking differences in climatic conditions from county to county. Those to the west tend to be much wetter than to the east and those to the north tend to be much cooler than to the south.

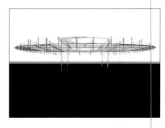

Above:
Elevation of the pavilion
The simple orthogonal steel frame generates the framework for the amorphous building.

Weather: Focus study 1

Name:
Blur Building

Location:
Yverdon-les-Bains, Switzerland

Date:
2002

Designer:
Diller Scofidio + Renfro

The Swiss Expo 2002 was intended to act as a laboratory to take a searching look at the future of our society, state and economy in the new millennium. This ambitious undertaking was organised within and around four towns and three lakes in western Switzerland. Each town had a particular theme: 'Power and Freedom' at Biel, 'Moment and Eternity' at Murten, 'Nature and Artificiality' at Neuchatel and 'I and the Universe' at Yverdon-les-Bains. At the edge of each town, by the shore of the lake, a small park of pavilions was constructed with an arm protruding to an artificial island, which was called an 'artplage' (art and beach).

A floating 'Artplage Mobile du Jura', unsurprisingly concentrating on 'Meaning and Movement', drifted between the four different sites and transported visitors between them.

Diller Scofidio + Renfro proposed to build not so much a building, but a cloud for the site at Yverdon. A 100 x 70 x 20-metre ball of drizzle would hover at about 25 metres above the lake. The cloud was made from filtered lake water that was forced as a fine mist through thousands of nozzles. They were attached to a large steel platform that was rooted to the bottom of the lake. The resultant fog created a cloud of mist, constructed from the lake itself and which changed and shifted in accordance with the particular weather conditions of the day. An integrated weather station monitored wind speed, direction and humidity and accordingly adjusted the 13 water pressure zones across the frame of the platform to maintain the dynamic form of the cloud.

The atomised water was designed to overwhelm the senses and create random moments of clarity and disorientation, dependent upon the movement of the dense fog. Sounds and smells were distorted by the lake water and any exposed clothing or skin was immediately soaked. The public were asked to wear bright blue waterproofs before approaching the long bridge to the cloud. Visitors then wandered the platform, encountering other disorientated blue ghosts within the dense cloud, until they found the stairs to the Angel water bar at the top where the spray was at its thinnest, high above the clouds and the lake.

'While the *Blur Building* is a visually striking architecture of atmosphere, it was also designed to be anti-spectacle. Contrary to immersive environments that strive to achieve high-definition visual fidelity with ever greater technical virtuosity, the *Blur Building* is decidedly low definition.'

Edward Dimendberg

Above:
The bridge
At particular times the building and the clouds merge together.

Facing page:
Interior of the pavilion
Visitors must wear a pale blue, waterproof cagoule while navigating the low-definition, immersive interior.

Above:
Aerial view of the pavilion
Water vapour billows from the pavilion.

Resources > **Weather** > Recycling

'The Santa Caterina site was a convent, a space where the sky opened. Truly, if you go to this large esplanade, you realise the scale of it in relation to the rest of the city and, where the market stands, the expanse of sky is enormous, then you can almost sketch what happens to the space in the old city, looking to the sky, looking upwards… For us it was important to conserve this idea of transparency, of a place you pass through…'

Benedetta Tagliabue

Top left:
Exterior of the market
The lattice panels between the undulating roof and the ground-floor walls allow for air movement through the market.

Left:
Detail of the panel
The timber screen is applied loosely to the exterior of the market.

Below:
The interior of the market
The dramatic oscillating roof encloses the vibrant market. Note the deliberately ill-fitting open screens.

Sustainability and the existing interior

Weather: Focus study 2

Name:
Santa Caterina Market

Location:
Barcelona, Spain

Date:
2004

Designer:
EMBT (Enric Miralles–
Benedetta Tagliabue)

The designer can consciously employ methods that take advantage of the existing climate within a remodelled building and design elements that provide for optimum environmental conditions.

Barcelona is a hot city and this market within the heart of the dense urban area benefits from a new roof that provides protection from the sun, while insulating the space and promoting the movement of fresh air through the building. The market is built on a large square over the ruins of a convent. Its creation provided an opportunity to open up the intense urban context of the site and link the previously closed space with the surrounding buildings and streets.

The market is characterised by a new, large, brightly coloured and distinct roof, which swoops and sways over the old walls and encloses the space. It is not a tight-fitting lid but a loose covering, flowing over the constraining market walls. The top of the roof is a colourful mosaic of abstracted images derived from the fresh fruit displayed on the market stalls below. The soffit of the roof is lined with timber and is supported by long steel trusses that connect to large concrete piers to the side of the space. The precise and relentless quality of the construction of the roof focuses the eye on the market stalls below and the eye-level displays of fish, fresh fruit and vegetables.

The open gap between the roof and the solid walls allows for the access of natural light and air movement within the enclosed space. The fretwork pattern encourages the air to speed up as it passes through the building, thus creating a breeze that serves to provide fresh air, cool the space and help remove any of the unpleasant smells associated with markets. The new roof provides the building with a distinct and well-defined identity; the gap between it and the existing walls provides the interior with clean fresh air.

Above:
Market entrance
Natural light is admitted into the building through the gaps in the roof.

Recycling old buildings, like recycling waste, is a process that is dependent on attitude and value. The question of value relates to how much of the recycled material is worth keeping, even though the process may be difficult and sometimes expensive, in order to extract something of worth.

Recycling: Focus study 1

Name:
Duisburg-Nord Country Park

Location:
Duisburg, Germany

Date:
1994

Designer:
Latz + Partner (Peter Latz), lighting by Fisher Park

Areas that may at first appear inaccessible and unwelcoming can be recycled to produce exciting and unusual results.

The Kommunalverband Ruhrgebiet of mid-western Germany is home to over five and half million people, in post-industrial towns such as Essen, Duisburg, Oberhausen and Dortmund. This was once the heavy industrial area of Germany producing much of its steel and mining coal. The international shift to cheaper sources of extraction and production has rendered much of the German steel and coal industry redundant. The closure of many of the plants led to a legacy of huge swathes of colossal yet obsolete buildings, packed with machinery and residing in land poisoned by the raw materials and processes of various industrial productions.

Demolishing these vast collections of buildings and structures has at times proved impossible and for many years, the process of recycling and reuse has been pursued. In certain instances, minehead buildings have been converted into cultural centres and business start-ups, gasometers have naturally been turned into art spaces and so on. The Thyssen steel works in Duisburg has been converted into an enormous public park. Visitors are encouraged to wander through the detritus of this once magnificent structure, to climb onto the towers and balconies that overlooked the massive furnaces and to marvel at the sheer scale of its operation.

The landscape has been delicately cleaned and replanted; now birch trees grow on the slag heaps, and surprising and rare foreign plants grow in bunkers having previously been hidden among the mineral and material deposits from other countries. The blast furnaces, coking plants, water towers and factories were recycled to become anything useful and appropriate; from an outdoor cinema to artists' studios. Even the local scuba diving club uses the water tanks for underwater practice. In the evenings, a dramatic lighting scheme by the stage designers, Fisher Park, illuminates the redundant towers, transforming them into huge sculptural figures, an apt gesture that symbolises their new 'environmentally friendly' credentials. The recycling of what was once an inhospitable and inaccessible place has transformed it into a postmodern interactive environment.

Sustainability and the existing interior

'Collective memory is a current of continuous thought still moving in the present, still part of a group's active life, and these memories are multiple and dispersed, spectacular and ephemeral, not recollected and written down in one unified story.'

M. Christine Boyer

Above:
The steelworks
Greenery and foliage grows amongst the industrial relics and detritus.

Left:
Theatre courtyard
Elements of the old building are recycled to facilitate creative activities.

Facing page top:
Photomontage site plan
The disused steelworks is an enormous found object within an industrial landscape.

Facing page bottom:
At night
The buildings are animated in a dramatic fashion by a night-time lightshow.

Facing page:
Interior of the agency
The organisation of the
original building has obviously
informed the arrangement
of the new interior.

Recycling: Focus study 2

Name:
TBWA\Hakuhodo

Location:
Tokyo, Japan

Date:
2007

Designer:
Klein Dytham architecture (KDa)

Interiors are usually created
to service a specific function
and the design of the space will
reflect the particular activities
happening within it. Sometimes
the functional requirements are
so specific, it is difficult to convert
or recycle without completely
losing the essence and honesty
of the interior.

However, the designer can
choose to retain the character
and indeed the obvious function
of a space and use it as the
starting point for the redesign.
One of the most outrageous
examples of the new and old
fitting together very well, but
each still retaining a distinct
and individual identity is KDa's
project for an advertising agency
situated within an operational
bowling alley.

In the dense, ever-changing
metropolis of Tokyo, KDa were
engaged to design the new
global headquarters for a recently
merged advertising company,
TBWA\Hakuhodo. This included
finding space for the 300-strong
workforce. The site was in an
eight-storey amusement complex
and the company had to share
their venture with a reception
for the gaudy gaming halls and
endure a still-working bowling
alley situated around them.

The designers adapted the
single-span, 30-lane bowling hall
into a studio for the company.
They worked within the existing
grain of the building using the
extended, timber lanes of the
alley for the distribution of work
and meeting spaces. Each lane
provided a long narrow length
of space for work activities and
the space between the lanes,
previously used for returning the
bowling balls, became circulation
routes. A folded office room was
positioned in each lane to provide
an element of private meeting
space for each team.

'New Office' design

The concept of the 'New Office' is
based on the idea that rather than sit in
a particular place within the office building,
a person might occupy the specific space
most suitable for the individual activity
that they are completing. Frank Duffy
developed this idea, and he called these
particular spaces the Den, the Hive, the Club
and the Cell.

Sustainability and the existing interior

Above:
Plan
The recycled building informs the organisation of the new.

Above right:
View across the office
The 'landscape' of various atmospheres encourages creativity.

Right:
Private spaces
Quiet rooms or 'dens' are used for intensive work. Note the hives of activity behind these spaces.

Weather > **Recycling** > Found object

The use and reuse of found objects can create connections with the past. The practice accepts the traditions, patterns and the language of either an existing site or the object. It suggests the application of an evocative approach to design that reads and then revises existing meaning within a place or an object. As a strategy for reuse, it is the appropriate use of appropriation.

Facing page:
Diesel Wall
The wall is used as a canvas for young creative artists.

Below:
Armani Wall
The existing building is used as a found object, on which Armani unashamedly advertises its label.

Found object: Focus study 1

Name:
Diesel Wall/Armani Wall

Location:
Milan, Italy

Date:
N/A

Designer:
N/A

A found object may be a small segment or detail that has become detached from a building. It could equally be a large, intact part of a structure.

Fashion brand Diesel is known for its support of young and creative talent. One of their most innovative initiatives is the annual competition to decorate the exposed gable end wall of an historic building near the San Lorenzo Church in the ever-fashionable Milan. The city is known as the world capital of the fashion industry and the contemporary architectural and design scene in Milan is just as inventive and competitive.

The wall is a highly visible found object and is positioned on the edge of the business district. The wall is not integrated into any other project; it has an autonomy, independent of its surroundings and although it is physically connected to the building behind it and therefore structurally supported by it, the 'Diesel Wall' is orientated in the opposite connection. Despite Diesel's altruistic assertions, the wall is a piece of advertising; it gains publicity for the company not just through the usual routes, but also through cultural reportage.

The 'Armani Wall', also in Milan, uses the same approach, but in a much more obvious manner. The company also appropriates a disused wall, again it is in a position to be viewed by many passers-by, but the approach that they take is much more blatant, although arguably, no less creative. The wall is a huge advertising hoarding. The latest design of each wall is always eagerly awaited in the fashion- and design-conscious environment.

'*Spolia* can be used as a method for creating form by appropriating objects where meaning is lost, inadvertently forgotten or has become obscured over time. This approach often provokes reflections, whether intentional or inadvertent, on the new use or meaning of the appropriated fragment.'

Graeme Brooker + Sally Stone

'The building had a life of its own, it had been added to, chopped about and changed throughout its history. We picked up on that idea. I'm just making another small input into the life of the building, which will be around long after I am gone. I was not trying to match what was already there, I just wanted to make sympathetic intrusions into the existing spaces.'

Joshua Wright

Found object: Focus study 2

Name:
Wapping Project

Location:
Wapping, England

Date:
2000

Designer:
Shed 54

Objects that display the history and nature of an interior can add character and worth to a space. The detritus and debris of our industrial past can imbue a place with a whimsical and nostalgic quality.

The approach that the designers took in this project was to appropriate the previous use of the building for decorative purposes, thus developing a link with its mechanised and engineered past. The Wapping Project is a gallery and restaurant that has been installed within a disused pumping station in East London. The designers treated the building with respect and an appreciation of its qualities and characteristics. They made only very minor sympathetic intrusions into the robust industrial structure but, more importantly, they did not attempt to imitate its style or use period details. The new and the old are obviously different but the new elements are of a similar magnitude to the original; they contain a suitably industrial language, which is derived from an understanding of the space. The turbine hall is Grade II listed; this included the pumps, turbines and piping from the 1890s. The designers deliberately preserved the 'found' qualities of the existing building, right down to the 186 miles of in situ piping that had been used to pass water to the various parts of London.

The designers realised that the best strategy was to do very little with the building and to leave its raw and industrial character intact. The turbine hall was retained in its rough and ready state with the turbines, switches and dials kept in place. Around these fixed elements the new restaurant was installed. The kitchen was housed behind a freestanding stainless steel screen and the bright yellow Verner Panton chairs self-consciously contrast with the olive green engines. The gallery was placed within the cleared-out boiler house and a new steel staircase, which takes its influences from the industrial architecture around it, links the restaurant to the gallery.

Sustainability and the existing interior

Right:
The turbine hall entrance
The arrangement of furniture reflects the orthogonal form of the building.

Below:
The pump house interior
The stainless steel kitchen is discreetly placed behind the disused engines.

Left:
The dining area
The bright yellow Verner Panton chairs contrast with the rusty green industrial machinery.

Recycling > **Found object** > Occupation

The designer can create an interior that is to be occupied in a sustainable manner. For example, occupants can be encouraged to use natural light rather than artificial, through the design of devices that throw light into the centre of the space. Heating and cooling can also be conducted in a more passive way in order to consume less energy. The manner in which space is used and inhabited and the extent to which the designer can control it is of vital environmental importance.

Right:
Section
The main body of the library hovers in the space behind the façade. The red arrows show the penetration of natural light and the blue arrows show the movement of cool, fresh air.

Above left:
Reception
The ground floor reception has a direct relationship with the exterior garden.

Left:
The reading room
Natural light and fresh air flow through the gap between the original façade and the new elements.

Top right:
The library
The front of the original building was retained to preserve the connection with the history of the area.

'Architects and engineers need to strive towards creating a better balance in buildings between resource use and performance. Mies van der Rohe's famous aphorism less is more should refer to reduced material and energy use and more comfort and value.'

Brian Edwards with Paul Hyett

Occupation: Focus study 1

Name:
The Women's Library

Location:
Whitechapel, England

Date:
2002

Designer:
Wright & Wright Architects

Even when working with old buildings, passive methods of controlling the conditions within the interior for the purposes of the building's new function can be applied and developed to encourage sustainability and energy efficiency.

The Women's Library was founded in 1926 by Millicent Fawcett, the celebrated women's rights campaigner, and contains one of the most comprehensive collections of literature about women's lives; from political activism to the minutiae of domestic living. The collection was brought together in 1977 and is now housed in a former public baths building in London's East End. The designers chose to retain the façade of the original building and construct a completely new structure behind it. Although the building, dating from 1846, was listed, the façade was remodelled and the new structure rears up six storeys behind it. The retention of the façade is a symbolic gesture in recognition of nineteenth-century women's work.

The project has been developed and constructed with a considered approach to its environmental impact. The main building is a masonry structure (with thermal mass) and most of the spaces are naturally ventilated. Wherever possible, the rooms are naturally lit and the building is highly insulated, thus reducing heating demands. The archive of the building is housed on the third floor and was contained within a secure, environmentally controlled atmosphere. The designers created a suspended 'black box', which floats freely away from the external walls of the building. Air movement is encouraged within the gaps around this enclosed space, thus bringing in air to cool the building. Wright & Wright and the engineers, Ove Arup, estimate that these energy-saving devices have reduced the need for complex air conditioning systems and have reduced the building's energy consumption by 20 per cent.

Found object > **Occupation**

'The empty stage of a room is fixed in space
by boundaries; it is animated by light, organised
by focus, and then liberated by outlook.'

Charles Moore
Gerald Allen
Donlyn Lyndon

Occupation: Focus study 2

Name:
Water Tower House

Location:
Shooters Hill, London, England

Date:
2000

Designer:
Loates-Taylor Shannon Ltd
(LTS Architects)

The reuse of unusual and striking buildings often leads to the design of unique and delightful interior spaces.

In this case study a 120-year-old Victorian water tower, residing in the grounds of a former hospital in south-east London, has been remodelled to create an unusual family home with an exceptional view.

The house is a two-storey pavilion, connected via a covered bridge to the eight new floors of the tower. The pavilion contains the entrance, kitchen, living/dining space and two en-suite bedrooms, while the previously empty shaft now contains extra bedrooms, bathrooms and a viewing platform, all of which are connected by a staircase – part existing cantilevered stone, part new steel – and a very neat hydraulic lift. The enormous cast-iron tank at the top of the tower, which, at its fullest, held 80 tonnes of water, was removed and has been replaced by a glass observatory. On a good day it affords views across London.

The warmth created by solar gain in the new glazed box at the top of the tower encourages air movement throughout the whole house. Cool air is dragged in at ground level and pulled though the kitchen. It then flows up the open staircase to replace the hotter air at the top. The tower retains its Victorian feel, the brickwork is clean and damaged terracotta mouldings were remade to match the old. There is even a shallow stepped pool between the tower and the pavilion to remind the owner of the previous function of the building. The designers have thus succeeded in creating a space for a completely new function without compromising sustainability, energy-efficiency or links to its context.

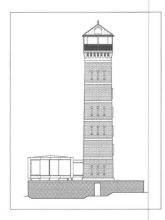

Above:
The house in context
The dramatic composition
of the house.

Facing page:
Elevation
Eighty tonnes of water were
at one time suspended on top
of this tower.

Top:
The observatory
The pavilion at the top of the
eight-storey tower provides
expansive views across London.

Above:
Interior of the pavilion
The pavilion is light and open in
contrast to the constrained and
enclosed quality of the tower.

Found object > Occupation

Sustainability and the new interior

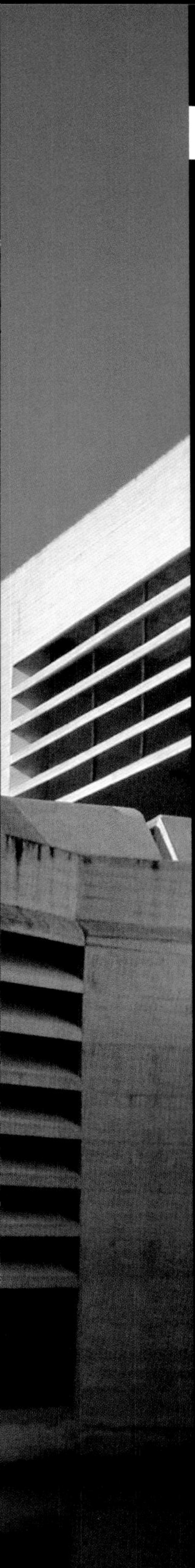

Sustainability is increasingly being seen as one of the most important design generators of the twenty-first century. When designing new interiors, these considerations must cover not just the way in which the interior space is designed but also the manner in which it is designed to be used. When working with new interiors, the designer will find that they have greater choice of resources and factors that influence the impact of weather, climate and other environmental factors. It is important that such factors are considered very carefully in order to ensure a sustainable and energy-efficient interior.

Name:
Pilar and Joan Miró Foundation
(see pp 132+133)

Location:
Palma de Mallorca, Spain

Date:
1993

Designer:
Rafael Moneo

Environmental awareness

There are many different aspects to the sustainable design of new interiors. The necessity to reduce the amount of energy used within everyday life has ensured that the designer has a responsibility to consider the manner in which a space is constructed and the way it is designed to be used. This covers the materials used and how they are sourced, the methods of construction and it also necessitates the design of a space that is both comfortable and environmentally balanced.

Resources

The design includes considerations of the materials; they can be used in a manner that creates as little pollution as possible – natural rather than man-made, for instance. The impact of transporting the materials should also be considered; heavy and bulky materials can be sourced locally, saving valuable energy for the lightweight or particularly precious or pivotal elements.

Weather

The design of the interior can take advantage of particular weather conditions; perhaps the designer can control the manner in which the sun or shade is admitted into the space or possibly allow vernacular solutions to influence the quality of the design.

Recycling

Recycling is another twenty-first century consideration: materials, and spaces or whole buildings can be recycled or reused. Obviously, there is more energy within the recycling process; the process of separating materials into the individual elements consumes more energy than simply reusing something.

Sustainability and the new interior

Found object

Found objects can enliven an interior, adding a sparkle of originality, drama or nostalgia.

Occupation

It is important that interiors are designed in such a way that users can employ energy-efficient living and working methods without limiting the building's viability.

Above:
Thermal baths, Vals, Switzerland (see pp 128+129).

The Brundtland Commission (convened by the United Nations in 1983) published its final report in 1987, *Our Common Future*. This defines sustainable development as 'development that meets the needs of the present without compromising the ability of future generations to meet their own needs.' This definition is deliberately imprecise and allows for many different readings and interpretations, while still providing a goal or standard to aspire to.

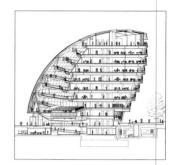

Environmental awareness: Focus study 1

Name:
City Hall

Location:
London, England

Date:
2002

Designer:
Foster + Partners

New techniques and technology are constantly helping designers to predict environmental conditions, facilitating more sustainable, environmentally sensitive and efficient designs.

Foster + Partners as a practice are very conscious of sustainable design and have acquired a reputation for creating buildings that are sensitive to environmental concerns. To this end they have developed their own variation on the accepted definition of sustainable design. The practice describes it as the process of creating buildings that are energy efficient, healthy, comfortable, flexible in use and designed for a long life.

The City Hall, or Greater London Authority Building, is located in a pivotal position opposite the tourist attractions of the Tower of London and London Bridge on the South Bank of the river Thames. The building is basically very simple; a series of stacked floor slabs enclosed by a steel and glass skin. But its unique shape is derived from sophisticated computer modelling software that has formalised the movement and impact of direct sunlight on the building. The computer calculated how the sun would strike the building on every day of the year and then adapted the design accordingly. Millions of calculations have then determined the shape and opacity of each piece of glass slotted into the skin of the building.

The south-facing side receives the most sunlight. The slipped stack of slab floors alleviates the problems associated with solar gain. Each overhangs the one below it and therefore provides a degree of shading.

The north-facing façade, which looks on to the Thames, receives minimal direct sunlight and therefore the glazing is unshaded. All the façades also have mechanically operated blinds to maximise shading.

Foster + Partners designed the building to minimise energy use and consume 75 per cent less energy than a traditional air conditioned office building. The building utilises natural ventilation systems and environmental control systems that incorporate naturally chilled groundwater drawn from boreholes that were sunk hundreds of feet below the building into the London Clay. The building contains a full-height 730-metre-long ramp that ascends the ten storeys and arrives at a rooftop viewing platform. Like the Reichstag in Berlin, which Foster also designed, the ramp not only gives dramatic views across the city but it also enables visitors to look down into the debating chamber and on to the politicians below.

Facing page:
Section
The protective overlapping floors
are clearly visible.

Right:
The building at night
The computer-generated, organic
shape of the building is a dramatic
element on the skyline.

Our Common Future
The Brundtland Commission's final report was
drawn up by an international group of politicians
in consultation with experts on environmental
development. It is thought of as a seminal document
because it brought to the attention of the world
the need to consider sustainable design and created
the context for environmental conservation.

Above:
Debating hall
The spiralling ramp offers a vast
and dramatic panorama of the
city and an intense, focussed view
of the debating chamber.

Introduction > **Environmental awareness** > Resources

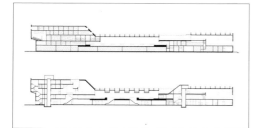

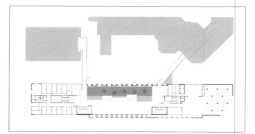

Sustainability and the new interior

Above:
Foyer
The shallow pool occupies
a vast amount of the space – note
the red booths on the far wall.

Left:
The cockle bowls
Rainwater drains from the
roof and into the bowls
of cockles where it is filtered
and then redistributed.

Top left:
Long sections
The interior landscape
is situated on the first floor.

Top right:
Plan
The first-floor foyer is
connected via bridges to
adjacent faculty buildings.

'Sustainable Design is a design philosophy that seeks to maximise the quality of the built environment, while minimising or eliminating negative impact to the natural environment.'

Jason F. McLennan

Environmental awareness: Focus study 2

Name:
Minnaert Building

Location:
Utrecht, The Netherlands

Date:
1998

Designer:
Neutelings Riedijk Architects

Modern interiors can sometimes become disconnected from the environment in which they are situated. The temperature and the quality of the light remain constant, with little or no recognition of the character of the different seasons.

The designers of the Minnaert Building wanted the occupiers to reconnect with and appreciate the changing nature of the natural world.

The striking Minnaert Building, with its enigmatic red 'veined' exterior, occupies the north-west corner of the Uithof University complex. Rem Koolhaas designed the masterplan and designated this area for the faculties of Earth Sciences, Physics and Astronomy, and Mathematics and Computer Science.

The environmental requirements of the building have been utilised to create an extremely unusual interior space. The foyer is at first-floor level; this is the social gathering space for the students and it also functions as a reception hall. It is lined on one side by bright red banquette seating, which is contained by a full-length screen with a Moorish motif cut from it. On the other side of the reception hall is a large pool of shallow water. This huge tank measures 10 x 50 metres, and is filled with rainwater that cascades into the hall through large openings in the roof. Each opening is positioned directly above a large dish of cockles. These creatures naturally purify the rainwater before it undertakes its next part of the journey. The pool is basically a large cooling mechanism for the building. The lecture halls, laboratories and computer rooms, along with lighting and people, generate lots of heat that, even in winter, requires permanent cooling. During the day the water is pumped from the hall and through the building to absorb the excessive heat, and then in the evening the water is pumped to the roof of the building and is chilled by the night sky.

The pool ebbs and flows throughout the different seasons of the year, reconnecting the students with the natural world. The natural light reinforces this as it enters the building through the rooftop openings. The atmosphere of the hall interior depends on the weather conditions outside, while the temperature of the building remains relatively constant as the water from the oasis at its heart is pumped around the building.

When designing new spaces, the interior architect is faced with a myriad of options and considerations regarding resources. The materials that a designer chooses to use have a huge impact on the efficiency and sustainability of a new project.

Resources: Focus study 1

Name:
Camlin Lonsdale Landscape Architects studio

Location:
Llangadfan, Wales

Date:
1990

Designer:
Francis Roberts Architects

The materials employed to construct a building may be directly derived from the local tradition or vernacular and they therefore establish a direct link with the immediate context. This can allow the form of the structure to be unique, but the continuity or permanence of tradition is retained.

This was the attitude taken by Francis Roberts Architects in the design of this studio in the heart of rural mid-Wales. The studio is situated on the edge of a small collection of farm buildings, yards and other agricultural spaces. This modest building was intended to integrate with its environment, to appear utterly natural and comfortable but at the same time to seem odd, to have an attitude, to express an extreme design sensibility. Agricultural buildings have traditionally had a functional brutality to them, they often look odd – their shape dictated by their purpose – and this provided the inspiration for the design. This building does not look agricultural though, it looks like a studio, only one in the middle of Wales. The structure is a rectangular box with a simple mono-pitch roof, but this simplicity belies a complexity of thought and organisation. The south-facing elevation, which is visible from the road, is deliberately kept short, the window is wide and narrow and reinforces the low, intimate quality of this façade. The mono-pitch leans back from this façade, again reducing the impact of the building. Windows in the roof admit controlled light into the upper floor while the eaves of the roof provide a certain amount of shade.

The opposite elevation of the building is sheer and full height, the windows are small and the effect is of a strong textured edge to the community of buildings. The west and east ends are simple and functional, the openings employ that particularly vernacular system of being positioned where they are needed rather than in a rational pattern or order.

The building is constructed and clad from local-sourced timber, in the same manner as the neighbouring barns. The interior has a control to it dictated by the order of the exposed structure and although it is busy and cluttered, the clarity of the building lends a serenity to the atmosphere. The focus is inevitably towards the landscape and certain openings offer views of specific features. The materials and the methods used to build them with tie the building to the particular landscape. It appears as if the studio could have always occupied this specific location, but it also seems far too contemporary to be real.

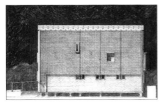

Left:
Pencil and crayon drawing
The slate roof and timber
boarding are rendered carefully.

Below left:
Concept sketches
The building is formed by its
relationship to the landscape.

Above:
Entrance to the studio
The building forms the edge
of the community.

Top:
Front of the building
The massive openings establish a direct relationship between the interior of the building and the landscape.

Above:
Entrance stair
The entrance stair is a dark and processional space.

Above:
Central pool
The roof lights allow the horizontal strata of the locally-resourced stone to be exposed.

Left:
The foot of the stairs
The darkness of the entrance area is relieved by the view through the interior to the light.

'What constitutes a sense of specific locality?
The constituent elements are, of course, reflections
of natural, physical and social realities. They
are expressions and experiences of specific nature,
geography, landscape, local materials, skills and
cultural patterns.'

Juhani Pallasmaa

Resources: Focus study 2

Name:
Thermal baths

Location:
Vals, Switzerland

Date:
1995

Designer:
Peter Zumthor

Using locally sourced materials and building techniques can benefit both the design and the environment.

Vals is a remote alpine village in the Valserrhein valley in the canton of Graubünden. The village grew up around Valser water, the mineral-rich natural spring water that was plentiful in the valley and has an extraordinary property whereby it turns bright red on exposure to the air. When the hotel that was positioned at the most bountiful spring became bankrupt, the rural community bought the building and commissioned local architect, Peter Zumthor, to create new thermal baths that would serve as a prominent destination in this isolated location. Zumthor is internationally renowned for his sensitive contextual approach, rooted in his understanding of the Swiss vernacular.

The baths are located in a steep-sided valley and embedded into the hillside. Indeed, the rooftop is a verdant green lawn upon which the hotel guests can wander, unknowing of what is beneath their feet. The entrance is via an underground tunnel link from the hotel reception. It is little more than a long concrete corridor, one side of which is stained by the mineral water pouring from wall-mounted copper pipes into a floor-mounted grill. Luxurious changing rooms are accessed from the other side. This hardly prepares the visitor for the scale, impact and beauty of the baths themselves.

The interior is much like a huge monolith that has been hollowed out from the hillside, creating caves, recesses and gulleys full of heated water for bathing, immersion and floating in. The baths are conceived as a series of stone caverns arranged around a central pool and a large outdoor pool. Between these spaces are plunge pools, petal baths, and even a deeply recessed sunken cavern with piped Gregorian chant.

The epic quality of the space is exaggerated by layer upon layer of Gneiss stone, which is used to clad the building both inside and out. It was cut from the local quarry and is totally appropriate for this environment. It is very sustainable to acquire heavy materials from sources close by, to reduce the amount of energy used in transportation. The slabs are long and thin, which helps to reinforce the massive and textured quality of this natural material. Light is used to dramatic effect in the interior. Thin slots cut into the roof allow vivid shafts of light into the space and wash the walls of stacked stone, heightening the drama of the interior space. The massive openings allow the visitor to visually connect with the landscape and the local materials employed within the construction of the building tie the building to its context.

With new interiors, the designer can take advantage of the particular weather conditions of an area. They can control the manner in which specific characteristics affect the building and thus enhance the quality of the interior space. In a hot climate, the designer can embrace the drama of the contrasting sun and the shade while in cooler climates the beauty of the rain or snow can be exploited.

Weather: Focus study 1

Name:
Flower kiosk

Location:
Malmö Cemetery, Sweden

Date:
1969

Designer:
Sigurd Lewerentz

Working on new-build projects allows the designer to take full account of the building's surrounding climatic conditions.

In one of his final and most influential projects, Lewerentz has combined the Swedish sensibility for reducing everything to its most simple with the minimal aesthetic of modernism. The flower kiosk is an incredibly uncomplicated structure that responds to the climatic conditions of the area.

Constructed from a minimal palette of materials: concrete, copper, glass, ceramics and laminated timber, the building was cast in concrete with untreated plywood formwork and therefore has a rough textured finish. The ridged mono-pitch roof is of copper and the windows are austere sheets of glass that are set into the concrete and so appear to be flush with the walls. The eaves of the roof are huge, creating an overhang that has many functions; it shades the front of the shop while throwing the rain and snow from this display area. It shields the building from the prevailing south-westerly wind and there is no need for a gutter – rainwater is allowed to just fall freely into the street and when it rains hard, it produces a beautiful curtain of water. The two windows have very different functions: to the south is a long display window, while the north-facing windows are set high up, next to the roof. This allows the even northerly light to flood across the ceiling.

The interior is equally functional. The floor is clad with ceramic tiles with broad protruding joints to minimise the risk of slipping. The walls are of untreated concrete with the looped electrical wiring carefully nailed to them. The ceiling has been clad with aluminium; this is to reflect the light into the heart of the space and the heat back into the room. Lewerentz has created a clean and simple building that responds to the needs of the users and the climate in which it positioned.

Above:
Exterior of the shop
The huge eaves of the roof protect the shop window.

Sustainability and the new interior

'Lewerentz's architecture is characterised
by a passionate realism combined
with a deep fascination for materials
and a strive for simplicity.'

Claes Caldenby
Jöran Lindvall
Wilfred Wang

Above:
Rear elevation
The crudely attached massive
windows throw constant
northerly light into the heart
of the interior.

Sustainability and the new interior

Above:
The reflection pool
A breeze, cooled by the water in the pool, is encouraged to blow through the louvred wall.

The stack effect
The stack effect uses the innate ability of air to rise as it is heated. If that air can be replaced with cooler air, then a natural circulation system is created. The incoming air can be cooled in a number of ways; a couple of the more simple are these: if the air is encouraged to pass over water, the dampness will lower the temperature; if the speed of the air movement can be increased, the breeze will act to cool the atmosphere.

Weather: Focus study 2

Name:
Pilar and Joan Miró Foundation

Location:
Palma de Mallorca, Spain

Date:
1993

Designer:
Rafael Moneo

The designer can create small, valuable elements within a much larger composition to affect the quality of a much larger space.

Within the hot climate of Mallorca, Rafael Moneo has used the natural qualities of light and water to create an atmosphere of coolness and character surrounding the paintings, drawings and sculptures of Joan Miró.

The architect delicately placed the foundation building between the almond grove that spreads out over the slope below the building and the artist's studio, which occupied the space immediately next to the road. The building is composed of a star-like volume to hold the art collection, and a linear element that contains the entrance, service areas and schoolrooms. There is a very tense relationship between these two contrasting elements.

The long thin building is placed on slightly higher ground than the splintered building; stairs within the foyer offer access to the lower gallery areas. This slight disconnection is emphasised by the pools of water, one of which is actually placed on the roof of the lower building. The landscaping also reinforces this difference; the upper level is organised in an orthogonal manner while the lower gardens are as dynamic as the star-like building.

The upper rectangular building has a south-facing colonnade integrated into it and from here the visitor has a magnificent view over the top of the gallery, across the island to the sea. This arcade also acts to help cool the building. This slender outside space shades the enclosed rooms, therefore reducing solar gain. The narrow shape encourages air movement, thus creating a slight wind that again aids cooling. This is supported by the louvres within the top half of the façade, they also stimulate air movement by encouraging the hot air to speed up as it rises through them. The pool of water directly below this area provides cooler air to replace this, and thus a small isolated stack effect is created. The movement of the water enhances the quality of the atmosphere; as it ripples it is reflected on to the underside of the colonnade and into the interior space. A small detail that creates a beautiful and effective environment also reduces the need for air conditioning for the comfort of visitors.

Top:
Covered walkway
The double skin provides a protected path between the interior of the building and the outside.

Above:
Exterior of the louvred wall
The louvres shield the interior from the hot sun and encourage air movement.

The reuse or recycling of materials can be regarded as an act of great sustainability. No new energy is needed to extract the natural materials or to form them. Reuse can also provide a symbolic and emotional historical link with previous occupants of a specific place.

Recycling: Focus study 1

Name:
Pulpit, Torcello Cathedral

Location:
Venice, Italy

Date:
Founded AD639, remodelled in the ninth century and rebuilt in the twelfth century

Designer:
Unknown

The creative reuse of small parts of a building suggests a relationship with history, with the collective memory, and reinforces the sense of belonging to a particular place.

The Venetians are consummate collectors and reusers of architectural fragments. In the field of ancient archaeology this practice is known as 'spolia', and involves the salvage of remnants from previous buildings that are reused and put to new use in other buildings.

Torcello is considered to be the oldest continuously populated island of Venice and once held the largest population of the republic. Today its population numbers below 100. The Santa Maria Assunta Cathedral was originally constructed in the seventh century and rebuilt in the eleventh century in the Byzantine style. It was all but abandoned in the thirteenth century as the growth of Venice, the silting up of its canals and the onset of malaria decimated Torcello's population.

The cathedral is famed for its intricate mosaic depicting the Last Judgement, which decorates the interior of the apse, and dates from the late eleventh century. It is also recognised for its pulpit, which has been fabricated from spolia. The steps are made from a series of architraves and other reliefs that have been simply cut to size to provide a clean edge for the balustrade. The fragments are remnants from the earliest church and, as such, are a direct link with the tenth-century structure. The reinstatement of these fragments was not an entirely arbitrary gesture and Patricia Fortini Brown explains:

'The restitution of the fragments to a certain degree of wholeness within the larger program calls attention to another occurring, and consummately Venetian, concern: to create a density of time within their major monuments through the employment of rediscovered relics.'[1]

The Torcello pulpit was constructed from a series of fragments that were treated in a simple, uncomplicated manner. This process does not attempt to disguise the original meaning; instead it is welcomed and the connection with history and time is embraced.

1
Fortini Brown, P. 1996.
Venice and Antiquity. New Haven, CT: Yale University Press

Left:
The view from the nave
The pulpit is raised up on
a variety of different columns.

Below:
The pulpit steps
The stairs are made from
saved fragments of building
ornamentation.

Spolia

Spolia is an archaic term that, until recently, was rarely
used outside of the study of Roman and medieval
antiquities. It describes the recycling of existing
architectural elements by incorporating them into
new buildings. It has lately become a more prevalent
term within contemporary interiors, and is used to
illustrate the process of removing elements from their
natural surroundings and placing them in an unusual
or different environment.

Above:
The pavilion corridor
A local musician wanders through the forest of stacked planks.

Right:
The pavilion edge
As it seasons, the wood exudes the smell of the Swiss pine forests.

'Resources which go into the manufacture of a building material can be retrieved and converted into a useful product at the end of the building's life.'

Brian Edwards

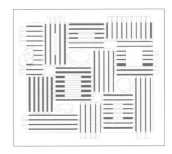

Recycling: Focus study 2

Name:
Expo 2000, Swiss pavilion

Location:
Hannover, Germany

Date:
2000

Designer:
Peter Zumthor

The designer has a responsibility to consider not just the expected life of a particular building or project, but also the future life or use of the materials embedded within that project.

This is just the attitude taken by Peter Zumthor in his project for the Swiss pavilion at the Expo 2000, held in Hannover. An exposition is a huge event, usually lasting for the whole summer, which different international cities take turns in hosting. They are designed to show off the creative and technical prowess of the participating nations. Exposition pavilions are usually temporary affairs, intended to symbolise the characteristics of a particular place and showcase its design prowess. The Swiss pavilion at the Expo 2000 was no different but it reveals a different type of European sensibility.

The pavilion was conceived as a labyrinth; a representation of woods and forests. The walls were formed from neatly stacked piles of unseasoned pine, cut from the Swiss forests and shaped in factories. No glue or nails were used to hold the building together. Instead, steel tension rods compressed the structure, allowing the green timber to become seasoned and, most importantly, to move as it dried out. The structure actually shrank by 120mm during the course of the exposition. The interior of the pavilion was a sensuous space, sweetly smelling and dark, with glimpses through the spaces between the timber planks and into the other rooms within the pavilion. Zumthor called the building a 'klangkorper', or 'sounding body'. Rain on the galvanised gutters on the roof created harsh sound within the interior and musicians were employed to wander through the enigmatic spaces playing traditional Swiss instruments.

But all expo buildings have a very limited lifespan and Zumthor considered this when he designed the building. The pine planks were little more than building blocks of a standard length and thickness. The expo process allowed them to become seasoned, while the steel tension rods ensured that they did not warp or become distorted. They were in prime condition to be recycled, to be used again within a new project.

Above:
Plan
The labyrinthine qualities of the interior are relieved by circular clearings in the timber 'forest'.

The reuse of a found object can greatly enhance the atmosphere and quality of a space. It can add a sense of nostalgia and remembrance to what would otherwise be a fairly anodyne place or it can add to an eclectic collection of elements and spaces. The found object may be totally suitable for the interior but from a different era or culture, making it subtly prominent, or it could be totally alien to the space, making a dramatic statement.

Found object: Focus study 1

Name:
Bunny Lane House

Location:
New Jersey, USA

Date:
2001

Designer:
Adam Kalkin (interior decoration by Albert Hadley)

Usually, self-designed architects' houses are an opportunity for the designer to develop unrealised ideas or obsessions.

Bunny Lane House by the architect and self-titled 'American anarchist', Adam Kalkin, is exactly that. The existing house on the rural site was a traditional New Jersey two-storey clapperboard house with shingle cladding. Rather than demolish this undistinguished building, Kalkin completely enclosed it within a corrugated steel shed.

A massive structure of the type usually found on an industrial estate, Kalkin viewed the house as a found object – a historical fragment that was left entirely intact within the portal frame of the shed.

The building has now become a strange collection of different types of enclosure; interior spaces within other interior spaces. This ambiguity has produced a new building that is both familiar while being equally surreal. What was once the front garden is now the living room and the front porch is the dining room. Walls and roofs that previously battled with the elements have, in a single stroke, now been relieved of that.

The scale and brutality of the shed contrasts strongly with the traditional quality of the original house, and also with that of the furniture, which is carefully positioned within the expanse of the ground floor. The shed was positioned to accommodate the house at the northern end and at the other, a tall, very modern, three-storey frame structure was inserted, containing offices and bedrooms. This leaves the 'courtyard' of a lounge in between the two internal structures. Huge sliding glazed doors allow natural light into this central space and reinforce the connection with the scale of the shed and the surrounding landscape. This design demonstrates an extraordinary approach to a found object that revives and enlarges a conventional structure in a most dramatic manner.

'We come from a culture of sampling. I'm just out there in the world picking out things and reusing things – sampling – from my experience and from what other people have already invested a lot of time and energy in. I think there's a tremendous amount of richness out there.'

Adam Kalkin

Above:
Inside the shed
The original house is just another object within the collection.

Top right:
The home at dusk
The openings within the shed reflect the adjacent interior functions.

Recycling > **Found object** > Occupation

Right:
Main gallery
The procession of objects rises from the new floor and hovers between earth and sky.

Below:
Museum façade
Studio Fuksas was commissioned to transform the stables of the villa into an archaeological museum.

Bottom:
Upper gallery
The upper gallery is a clean, contemporary insertion within the elegantly decaying gallery space.

'The atmosphere of all preserved buildings is
unavoidably instilled with the qualities of fetish.
The idea of alteration is to offer an alternative
to preservation or demolition, a more general strategy
to keep buildings beyond their time.'

Fred Scott

Found object: Focus study 2

Name:
Tuscolano Museum

Location:
Frascati, Italy

Date:
2001

Designer:
Massimiliano Fuksas

Simple methods of environment control can be used in even the largest of spaces.

This is the approach that Fuksas has taken at the Tuscolano Museum. The seventeenth-century Villa Aldobrandini and gardens occupy a prominent location on the hillside town of Frascati overlooking Rome. Carlo Maderno designed the building; he was also the architect of the façade of St Peter's Basilica, which can be seen from the villa's hilltop location. Studio Fuksas were commissioned to transform the stables of the villa into a museum for archaeological exhibits, temporary exhibition space, auditorium and administrative offices.

The main hall of the stable holds the exhibition space while a new floor inserted into the hall accommodates the temporary exhibition space. Initially, the stables were sensitively cleaned and then restored, traces of the previous occupancy were retained within the marks, dents and other signs of wear on the walls. The insertions were distinct from the old building; the new floor is constructed from steel and concrete, while new stairs are from steel and timber. In order to accommodate the services (toilets, a lift and emergency stairs) a prominent yet modest block was placed in the middle of the building, thus neatly dividing the high, double-height front hall of the stable from the smaller vaulted room at the back.

But the most striking element of the new design is the manner in which the designers have displayed the exhibits of the museum. The archaeological artefacts are arranged in a long procession through the middle of the space. They are secured behind sheets of toughened glass over two and a half metres high, which are set into a recessed channel in the polished concrete floor. Each object is displayed on a slender bronze stand designed by Massimo Mazzone and is illuminated by a tiny hanging spotlight. The objects appear to be suspended in mid-air, hovering between earth and sky. This is symbolic of the journey that these artefacts have endured; each object has been removed from the ground and it almost appears as if it was still carefully preserved there, as if the earth has just been removed to reveal the fragility of the object. The exhibits act as found objects and the delicacy of their display reminds the visitor of their history. This is a very appropriate gesture in a building already imbued with the impact of time.

The designer can work to ensure that the interior spaces are occupied in a manner that is environmentally conscious. Various techniques can be employed to reduce the amount of energy consumed by the occupants; from encouraging the entry of adequate natural light, to the control and manipulation of solar gain.

Occupation: Focus study 1

Name:
Scottish Parliament Building

Location:
Edinburgh, Scotland

Date:
2004

Designer:
EMBT (Enric Miralles – Benedetta Tagliabue) and RMJM

Simple methods of environmental control can be used, even in the largest of spaces. Complex and large buildings that are to be used for multiple functions and by large numbers of people will need to make use of the most efficient and up-to-date environmental and climatic control strategies.

The winning competition entry for the New Scottish Parliament building by EMBT was distinguished by its close relationship with the topography of the site and the landscape of the country it represents.

The building is located within the ancient urban landscape, at the bottom of the Royal Mile in the old town, opposite the Royal Palace at Holyrood and next to Arthur's Seat and Salisbury Craggs. The building literally grows organically out of the context, connecting to the existing buildings on the site. It contains a new debating chamber, media buildings, four towers of committee rooms, staff offices and homes for the new Scottish Members of Parliament. Surprisingly, over half of the site is landscaped; a series of private and public gardens with paths and ponds completes the organic nature of the building.

The chamber is the grandest space of the building and is designed as a huge semi-circle. Its roof is a complex construction of laminated Scottish oak beams and steel reinforced tension rods. The hammer-beam roof of the 1639 Parliament building inspired it and its complex structural gymnastics provides the SMPs with an unobstructed view of the main speaker.

The debating chamber sits at the heart of this complex and is directly connected to the free-flowing organic circulation space. This has the twelve signature upturned-boat-shaped roof lights, which provide one of the most dramatic top-lit interiors of the building. This is a key space within the building: it is much more than a simple lobby; it is generously large and provides for a variety of different activities to take place, from informal meetings and television interviews, to the taking of refreshments and more formal receptions. This space was conceived with great environmental concern; the natural light is dominant, thus reducing the need for extensive artificial fittings. Warming sunlight is also encouraged to enter, to supplement the mechanical heating. The occupants are encouraged to extensively occupy this crucial space whenever possible, rather than shut themselves away in their individual offices, thus reinforcing the contemporary notion of transparency and openness.

Above:
The debating chamber
The elaborate and complex roof structure ensures unobstructed views across the Scottish oak-lined debating chamber.

Facing page:
Rear of debating chamber
Even the recesses of the chamber are flooded in natural light.

Above right:
The context
The building forms a new addition to a number of important urban landmarks.

Right:
Plan
The new building is very much a part of its context and it links the existing buildings on the site.

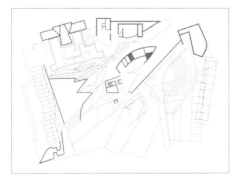

Found object > Occupation

Occupation: Focus study 2

Name:
Balornock Bowling Club

Location:
Glasgow, Scotland

Date:
2005

Designer:
Studio KAP Architects

It is often possible to combine user comfort with aesthetics to produce both dramatic and energy-efficient designs.

Studio KAP Architects' design of the new Balornock Bowling Club clubhouse combines a sensitivity to environmental concerns with a series of uncomplicated functional spaces.

The long narrow structure hugs the west side of the bowling green, without dominating or overshadowing it. It is raised up above the green on the existing banked ground, with its major spaces overlooking the competitive lawn, but is deliberately kept low and unassuming. The simple contemporary style is a modern interpretation of the classic bowling club pavilion.

The interior is equally minimal; the clean, plain walls and wooden floor do not distract from the view through the huge picture window. The focus of the space is the outside, towards the bowling green.

The large window also allows for plenty of light to penetrate into the depth of the interior spaces, especially in winter when the low sun is very welcoming.

The overhanging eaves provide sufficient shade in the summer to stop over-heating; the length of the projection is enough to stop solar gain, while also providing shade for the spectators outside the building. The cutback within the façade at the entrance also serves as a veranda, allowing for members to take a drink outside when the weather permits. The openings and other significant elements within the building are clad in timber and thus stand out as important events within the rendered façades.

The whole simple economic structure is generated by and is totally sympathetic to its context and it makes, at the same time, a modest contemporary statement about environmental design.

'The model for sustainable design is nature itself. Nature is efficient and effective by design, essentially producing no waste. In contrast to nature the process by which we design, make and use resource is linear in nature, using energy and producing waste at every step.'

Mary Ann Lazarus
Sandra Mendler
William Odell

Right:
Timber seat
The architectural façade accommodates a number of different types of activities.

Below:
Front elevation
The pavilion responds directly to the bowling green.

The designer can use individual elements to control the quality of interior space. These elements will have a relationship with the whole building and with each other. This will help to regulate and inform the character of the building and the interior. These specific objects, placed inside or outside, can help control the acoustic, visual, environmental and spiritual characteristics of the place, as well as helping develop three-dimensional relationships within and without the building.

Name:
Le Fresnoy Art Centre
(see pp 158+159)

Location:
Tourcoing, France

Date:
1998

Designers:
Bernard Tschumi Architects

Sustainability and the new interior > Elements that control space

Exterior control
Objects that exist outside of the interior can work to alleviate problems caused by the surrounding environmental conditions. These might include mechanisms such as shading devices and environmental barriers as well as natural elements and their relationship with the interior.

Interior control
The placement and use of internal mechanisms such as materials, found objects, shading devices and circulation devices can exert control and influence on the qualities of a space.

Above:

Qiora store and spa,
New York, USA (see pp 168+169).

Elements placed outside a space can have a direct influence on the quality of an interior in a number of practical ways. Features that alleviate poor weather conditions, control the entry of excessive sunlight or provide effective insulation can all contribute to the creation of a pleasant and comfortable interior space.

Exterior control: Focus study 1

Name:
Maison de Verre

Location:
Paris, France

Date:
1928

Designer:
Pierre Chareau and
Bernard Bijvoet

Elements placed on the outside of the building can facilitate maximum exposure to light. This is particularly useful for buildings that are situated in dark, tight and crowded environments.

The early twentieth-century desire for transparency, openness, cleanliness and light led Dr Dalsace, a leading French gynaecologist, to convert the bottom two storeys of a four-storey Parisian town house into his medical clinic and private house. The furniture and interior designer, Pierre Chareau, designed the project with the help of Dutch architect, Bernard Bijvoet. It epitomises the optimistic, inventive era in which it was constructed.

The house sits in a courtyard that is accessed from the main street by a narrow alley. The top two storeys of the house were supported on a massive steel beam and column structure, and then a glass brick screen wall was cantilevered clear of them to create a free façade. This glass brick curtain wall illuminates the double-height interior, a huge modern living room – a very radical and progressive move at the time.

It is the elevation that characterises the house, and indeed, gives it its name. The glass bricks are laid in four-brick-wide panels and they establish a 91cm grid that controls the dimensions throughout the entire interior design of the scheme. During the day the façade facilitates the admittance of natural light into the interior. At night the reverse effect happens and tantalising, distorted glimpses of the artificially illuminated interior space are projected to the outside world. This was a groundbreaking project that perfectly caught the prevailing need for simple, clean and lucid design.

Facing page:
The courtyard elevation of the house
The projecting glass screen is suspended in front of the façade of the original building.

Below:
Axonometric
The drawing shows the double-height living space behind the new screen.

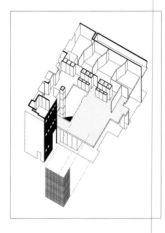

'Chareau did not aspire to the "integrated whole"
that is generally judged a hallmark of fine architecture.
Instead he chose to work additively, addressing
difficulties piecemeal as they arose and often finding
striking solutions to them – hence the exposure
of the services and the Maison de Verre's fascination
for subsequent generations of designers.'

Richard Weston

'A building modifies the external natural environment by moderating the climate and providing protection and shelter, and designers need to understand how the external climate, the building fabric and the human body interact.'

Energy Research Group

Elements that control space

Exterior control: Focus study 2

Name:
Santa Caterina market housing

Location:
Barcelona, Spain

Date:
2006

Architect:
EMBT (Enric Miralles–
Benedetta Tagliabue)

Shading devices can be used to reduce daytime glare and heat gain, and night-time heat loss from the interior. Overhangs, canopies, light shelves and blinds or louvres are all exterior elements that can help to do this.

The overhang, if orientated towards the south can alleviate the intensity of the hot summer sun (in the northern hemisphere), but it will offer little protection from the low winter sun, if any is needed. The canopy can offer temporary protection to the interior, but it is usually far too fragile to withstand bad weather. The light-shelf works in two ways: it is placed quite high up within an opening so that light bounces off the top of it and is reflected into the heart of the interior space. The horizontal shelf also acts as a barrier so that direct sunlight is not admitted into the space immediately next to the window. Fixed horizontal louvres can stop the high southerly sunlight but they offer little protection from the more flat east or westerly light. Moveable louvres and screens can be mechanically positioned to follow the sun and block out all of the sunlight.

The slightly warped, orthogonal form of the housing next to the Santa Caterina market contrasts strongly with the flowing roof canopy of the market building. The contextual deformations of the housing appear responsive and natural in the tight urban landscape. The walls are sheer and white with an apparently arbitrary splattering of windows arranged on them. This simplicity is reinforced by the manner in which the openings are treated. Each window is covered with an austere and unpretentious wooden louvred panel, mounted on runners. When necessary, these can slide in front of the openings to stop direct sunlight from overheating the interior, while still encouraging air movement through the gaps between the individual blades. This offers a solution that is both simple and passive.

Top:
Screen
The louvres protect the interior space from the more damaging climatic elements.

Above:
New meets old
The contemporary language of the new building is derived from the form of the existing apartment blocks.

Facing page:
The flats from beneath the market canopy
The position of the orthogonal blocks is juxtaposed against the billowing roof of the market building.

Left:
Chapel of Resurrection
The scale of the porch is huge and overwhelming.

Below:
Side elevation
A small slither of space separates the porch from the building.

Right:
St Marks, Björkhagen
The modernist curved canopy
protects the area in front
of the church and is slightly
detached from the building.

Exterior control: Focus study 3

Name:
Chapel of Resurrection and
Church of St Mark

Location:
Stockholm and Björkhagen,
Sweden

Date:
1925 and 1956

Designer:
Sigurd Lewerentz

An external porch can offer
many benefits to an interior
space, both formal and
environmental. The covered
entrance, portal or portico can
signal the entrance. It is often
unclear in modern buildings
where to get in! With their pursuit
of minimalism and cleanliness,
the actual position of the entrance
is sometimes ambiguous.

The portico can obviously
demonstrate the hierarchy
that exists, and reveal
the natural order of the building.
Psychologically the porch will
also offer a moment of thought
and reflection as the visitor
moves from the outside to inside;
it provides a significant second
to adjust to a pace of life that
is slower, quieter and more
gentle. This course is reversed
on the way out of the building.
The covered entrance also
offers a degree of environmental
protection; it shelters the visitor
from the rain or the sun and
keeps a certain amount of
wind from them. It also aids
the environmental control of the
building, protecting a potentially
vulnerable opening within
the façade.

Illustrated are two examples
of work by Sigurd Lewerentz,
a Swedish architect who
practised for much of the
twentieth century. The first
is the Chapel of Resurrection
in Stockholm. The portico
entrance is slightly detached
from the main building; it is
composed of eight columns with
a pediment roof. The language
is highly appropriate to the
stripped classical style prevalent
in Scandinavia at the time.

St Mark's in Björkhagen,
Sweden, was designed much
later in a modernist style.
The portico is also detached
but it is composed of a broken,
undulating plane supported
by massive double columns.
It is obviously sympathetic
to the quite brutal and spare
nature of the brick building.
Although they were designed
some thirty years apart, the
two examples of porticos
exhibit very similar protective
characteristics.

'I dream of a building with books, books, and more
books, and with beautiful round reading rooms.
A building where you can see, feel, and smell books…
The aura and the new library must form the heart,
they must come to be situated in a park like landscape.'

Francine Houben

Elements that control space

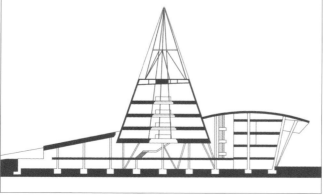

Above:
The library interior
The cone dominates the large
hall. Note the reference book
stack on the right.

Left:
Section
The cone interrupts the
flowing landscape on the
roof of the library.

Exterior control: Focus study 4

Name:
Delft University of
Technology Library

Location:
Delft, The Netherlands

Date:
1997

Architect:
Mecanoo Architects

A series of external elements
can work together to control the
environment within the interior.

The library at Delft University
of Technology is a modest and
unpretentious building situated
among a complex of overbearing
brutalist structures. The real
scale of the building is hidden,
it is a huge underground space
concealed beneath a flowing
landscape. The roof is an inclined
grass plane, a new park for
the students.

The vast foyer space below
was conceived as the meeting
place for the campus. It is
edged with inclined glass
walls and supported by slender,
white-painted, steel columns.
A huge cone rises through the
open hall, pierces through
the green and rises to 40 metres
above the ground. This is the
quiet working element and
contains four levels of study
spaces connected by a helical
stair. It is supported on splayed
steel columns, is naturally top-lit
and allows the library users to find
somewhere quiet away from the
expanse of the library hall.

The cone dominates the interior
but another crucial element
is the four-storey, steel-framed
bookcase that contains over
80,000 general reference books.
It is situated at the highest
point within the space and
serves as a barrier between the
reception hall and the service
areas. The thick greenery of the
roof provides excellent insulation
and soundproofing and acts to
keep the interior cool in summer
and warm in winter. Rainwater
is also drained from the roof
and used to aid the heating
or cooling of the building.
Triple-glazed façades also aid
the environmental strategy
of the building and the 140mm
cavity between the panels of
glazing allows air to be moved
in and between the glass screens.
As such, a sympathetic and
contextual approach has
produced an interior of great
drama and wit.

Above:
Under the cone
The tranquil space beneath
the cone provides a space for
private study.

Exterior control: Focus study 5

Name:
Le Fresnoy Art Centre

Location:
Tourcoing, France

Date:
1998

Architect:
Bernard Tschumi Architects

Elements that provide environmental control need not be small, modest structures; they can also be massive, generous statements of intent.

The French architect, Bernard Tschumi, has used a single huge element to solve a number of contextual and environmental problems at Le Fresnoy in Lille, northern France, and in so doing has created a series of buildings and spaces that encourage creativity and interaction.

The original site consisted of a series of disparate crumbling and decaying buildings that were constructed as some sort of holiday camp. Indeed, one of the buildings (an auditorium) was called the 'Fun Palace'. The collection of existing buildings resembled very closely the requirements of the new school; in fact, the directors apparently assumed that they would need very little work to accommodate the arts school. However, the individual buildings were considerably more dilapidated that was foreseen, and so Tschumi arrived at a solution that retained the atmosphere of the holiday camp and combined it with the creativity of an artistic institution.

Tschumi's approach was to restore and repair the existing buildings and then cover them with a giant roof. This served not only to protect the site, but also to unite the whole campus. The new structure over the roofs of the old buildings provides space for service equipment, air conditioning units, electrical wiring, maintenance stairs, and a series of new catwalks and public walkways. These give views across the roofs of the existing buildings and into the various rooms and spaces. This created a sort of village atmosphere within the school with more than enough functional space for the prescribed activities, as well as a collection of extraordinary interstitial spaces that were neither inside nor outside. They were not actually within any of the buildings, but were still within the shelter or enclosure of the giant roof. These extra, or accidental, rooms were intended for student interaction and relaxation.

A single huge new element that solves a number of environmental problems has in this way united a series of contrasting components and created some extraordinary spaces of unexpected atmosphere.

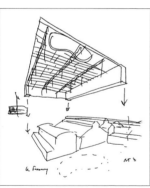

Top:
The junction between the roof and the old building
Vertical circulation is placed at this crucial pivotal point between the two buildings.

Above:
Designer's sketch
This drawing shows the concept of a protective roof over a community of existing buildings.

'The architecture of pleasure lies where concept and experience of space abruptly coincide, where architectural fragments collide and merge in delight, where the culture of architecture is endlessly deconstructed and all rules are transgressed.'

Bernard Tschumi

Above:
Under the roof
The view from an interstitial space, across the rooftops of the old buildings.

A number of obvious interior atmospheric qualities can be manipulated. The nature of the space, intensity of the light, whether it is natural or artificial, the quality of the air and the purity of the acoustics are all factors that can be considered to the enhancement of the space.

Facing page:
Entrance view from the alley
The ceiling-mounted air conditioning system reinforces a sense of movement through the bar.

Interior control: Focus study 1

Name:
Bar Ten (see also pp 038+039)

Location:
Glasgow, Scotland

Date:
1991

Designer:
Ben Kelly Design

The control and flow of air through a space, either naturally or mechanically, is an important consideration in the design and construction of an interior.

Nightclubs, bars and pubs invariably rely on mechanical extraction. They are habitually hot and crowded places with, until the beginning of the twenty-first century, heavily polluted atmospheres. Usually air conditioning units, HVAC ducts and fans are hidden out of site, stored behind a suspended ceiling or dropped soffit. However, the designer can deliberately expose these units for decorative effect. The ducts and grills of the system may be part of the aesthetic of the space, used not only to control the air in a room but also used to aid the direction and dynamic of the interior.

In the small, narrow interior of Bar Ten in Glasgow, Ben Kelly accentuated the form of the room by placing exposed HVAC ducts above the long, granite-topped bar. All the fitted furniture and fixtures in the space co-operate to recognise and heighten the long, narrowing shape of the room. The bar, foot rail, drinks display, banquet seating, air conditioning unit and even the floor pattern continue the spiralling journey that started in the main street some 50 metres away, along the narrow alley, through the bar and into the deep interior of the space. The galvanised steel box of the air conditioning system is just one of a number of elements that controls the atmosphere and nature of the space.

Ben Kelly Design
Ben Kelly Design were formed in the mid-1970s by Ben Kelly. The practice has a reputation for producing innovative, high-profile, post-industrial interiors, such as the legendary Manchester nightclub the Haçienda, the Design Council offices in London and, more recently, a series of 'GYMBOX' fitness clubs. The Ben Kelly Design philosophy is to retain the best features of the site while utilising an eclectic palette of materials, textures and finishes.

Elements that control space

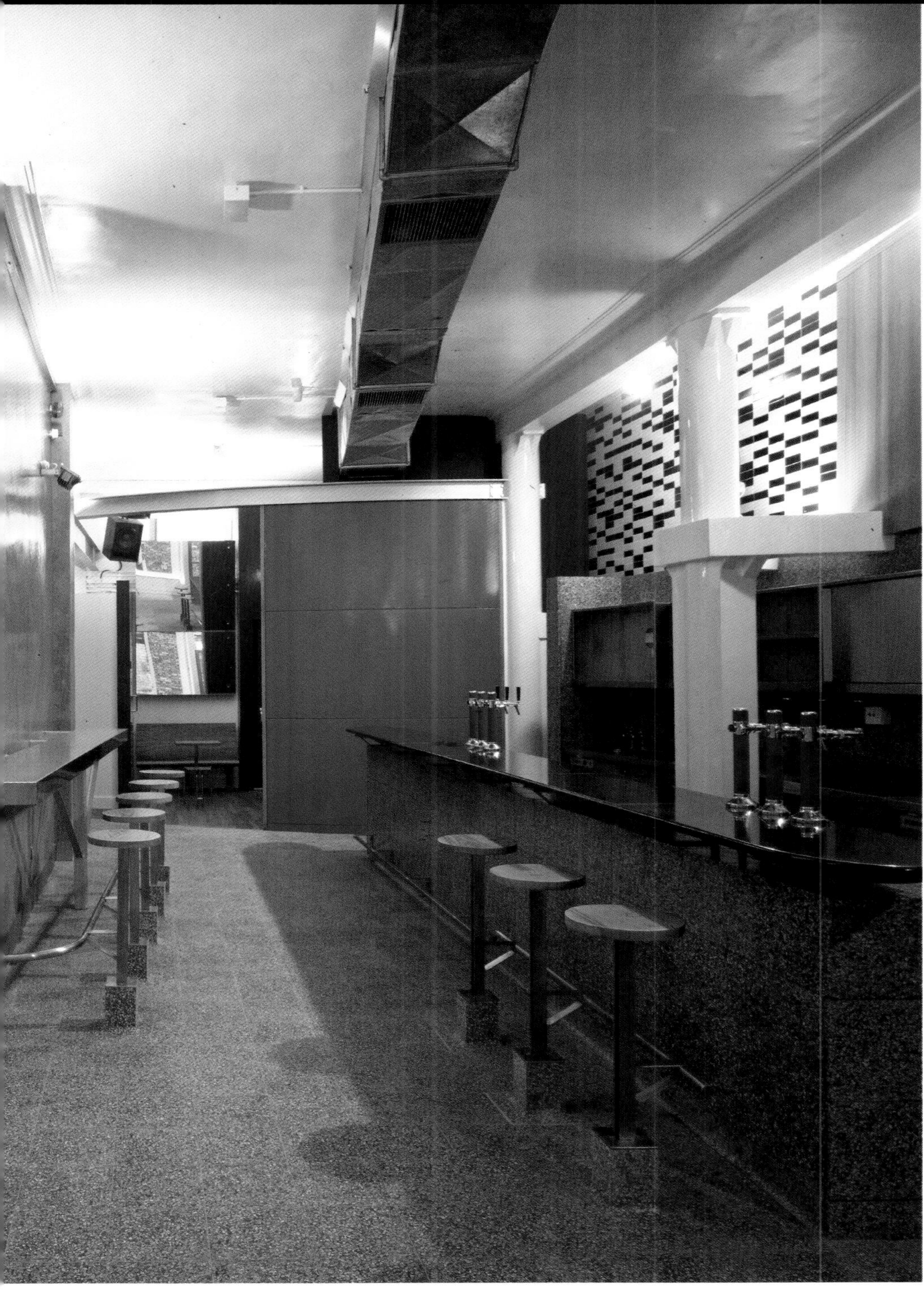

Above:
Auditorium interior
Elements of the Welsh landscape are reflected in the textured grey fabric on the seats.

Left:
Auditorium seat
The fabric is absorbent and acts as an acoustic baffle.

'We can use sound as a building material for spatial design along with light, shadow, or concrete.'

Bernhard Leitner

Interior control: Focus study 2

Name:
Welsh Millennium Centre

Location:
Cardiff, Wales

Date:
2004

Architect:
Capita Percy Thomas with Arup Acoustics and Bute Fabrics

The acoustic performance of an auditorium is a primary consideration when designing a theatre or performance space. Whether large or small, the shape and materiality of the space must be analysed and considered to attain the best acoustic dynamic. The basic concerns are sound reverberation time, echo and absorbency. Specialist acoustic engineers can be consulted so that the optimum form and material are proposed and therefore the best possible sound is achieved from the space.

The Welsh Millennium Centre is located next to a dry dock in the Cardiff Bay development area. It is dominated by an enormous steel dome, covered with copper oxide to be able to withstand the harsh sea air. The dome accommodates the main auditorium space and this is where opera, ballet and dance performances are held. The building also contains other smaller performance spaces and rehearsal studios along with shops, restaurants and offices for Welsh arts organisations.

The building is conceived as homage to all things Welsh and, naturally, Wales is both the inspiration and the source of all of the materials. The most prominent example of this is the exterior, which is clad in horizontal bands of local slate. The seating in the main auditorium has been created in a joint collaboration between the architects, engineers and Bute Fabrics. Bespoke fabrics were created for the seats to not only echo the inherent Welsh identity of the building but also to function as acoustic baffles within the auditorium. The colours of the fabrics were designed to imitate the atmospheric image of a Welsh beach, and were arranged on the seating in horizontal lines in order to evoke an image or simulacrum of the layers of slate that clad the exterior of the building.

Above:
The gallery
The Bohen Foundation in a state of transition.

Right:
Private room
The cut openings reveal the fragility of the crate.

Above:
Conceptual diagram
The crates slide through the structural logic of the building.

Left:
The library
The crates are cut and folded to create different types of space.

Elements that control space

Interior control: Focus study 3

Name:
Bohen Foundation

Location:
New York, USA

Date:
2002

Designer:
LOT-EK

The designer may respond to a particular context by using the same colloquial language, but in a contemporary or radical manner. In this project, the designers have emulated the dialect of the surrounding area, but misrepresented, enhanced and embellished it.

The raw atmosphere of the meatpacking district in downtown Manhattan provides the context for the Bohen Foundation, an institution that provides space for exhibiting contemporary art that does not lend itself to traditional white-walled galleries. The foundation is based in a large warehouse that was once a printing factory. The ground-floor and basement areas are clean, raw and unfinished and where possible, a mesh floor has been installed to create a double-height open space with maximum flexibility for the more unusual artworks.

The factory space is dominated by a grid structure of columns and beams, a structural system that has influenced the redesign of the interior. Twelve shipping containers have been inserted into this grid – the size of the crates conveniently conforms to the size of the bays. These vivid and industrial objects contain the traditional gallery facilities such as the offices, a bookshop, video room and a reading space and each also stores five foldable wall panels. The position of these containers is not fixed; they are supported on runners set into tracks in the floor. Movement is limited to the length of the floor tracks; the crates can slide parallel to each other through the length of the space.

However, the panels are much more flexible. They can be swung through the space with much more ease and dexterity. And thus, depending on the position of the two types of elements, a whole series of different types of spaces can be created. The character of the crates and screens is totally appropriate to the language of the industrial, warehouse-like gallery space. It is a contemporary, uncompromising place for radical and fashionable people.

LOT-EK

LOT-EK were formed in 1993 by Ada Tolla and Giuseppe Lignano. In 1989 the designers moved from Italy to New York to complete their education and were stunned by the harsh industrial landscape of the city – a reaction that, subsequently, has had a considerable impact on their work. They use found objects such as shipping containers, petrol tanks, steel sinks and industrial cast-offs – even the fuselage of a jet engine – to create buildings, interiors and objects. As Tolla states 'It's the philosophy of the ready-made bricolage, of improvising and using your intuition.'[1]

1 Hudson, J. 2007. *Interior Architecture Now*. London: Laurence King Publishing

Exterior control > **Interior control**

Left:
Gallery foyer
The pure white box at the top
of the gallery.

Interior control: Focus study 4

Name:
Sackler Galleries, Royal Academy
of Arts

Location:
London, England

Date:
1991

Designer:
Foster + Partners

Natural light can give great
benefit to the atmosphere
of a space. It can promote
movement, illuminate particular
spaces and define form.

Foster + Partners used the very
basic qualities of filtered natural
light to encourage circulation
within a tight vertical space.

The Royal Academy of Arts
is a complicated set of buildings
and structures that have been
added to or extended over
14 times since the construction
of the original country house
in 1665. The space between
Sir John Denham's original
building, Burlington House, at
the front facing Piccadilly, and
the garden house, completed in
1867 by Sydney Smirke,
is about four and a half metres.
This gap, Foster reckoned,
was just enough to insert an
autonomous circulation system,
which would provide access
to the new Sackler Galleries
on the top floor of the complex.

The steel and glass staircase
and lift lead the visitor from the
dark depths, deep within the
interior of the Royal Academy,
and up into the bright white light
of the Sackler foyer.

This is a pure, rectangular, white,
glass room that is perched on
top of the cornice of Burlington
House. The laminated glass
box uses a layer of white
PVB, sandwiched between the
panels of glazing, to obscure
the particularly poor view, filter
the natural light and control
solar gain. Natural light floods
through the glass and into the
slot of circulation space, down
past the edges of the floor
and through the translucent
glass stair tread. The box takes
its structural support from
the surrounding buildings and
connects the two buildings
together, enclosing the gap
to make a weather-sealed interior
environment out of what was
previously a draughty external
gap. This entrance sequence
is a contemporary statement
within a classical space.

Elements that control space

'In 1991, [we] completed an addition to the Sackler Galleries, within the Royal Academy of Arts in London. Laminated glass played an important part in the design of the glazed reception area. It was important to find an affordable, safe product to form the enclosure, which allowed daylight to flood into the space between the two original buildings.

'Normal float glass incorporates iron, which gives glass its green color. But this would also affect the color of daylight inside the gallery. We could not afford optically white glass and instead found a reliable source of glass where the iron content was much lower, thus helping to solve the problem. We used laminated glass for both safety considerations and because, by incorporating a white PVB interlayer, we could control solar gain and diffuse daylight.'

Rob Partington

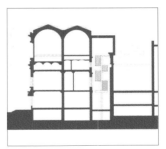

Above:
Section
The reception area for the foyer rests on top of the coping of the original building.

Left:
Vertical circulation
Visitors are moved from the dark depths of the building to the light.

Exterior control > **Interior control**

'Curtains…embody many of the tensions and prejudices that have divided interior designers and architects since the emergence of the professional decorator in the late nineteenth century. Here the hard walls designed by the architect meet the soft fabric that is the decorator's trademark.'

Joel Sanders

Above:
Designer's concept sketch
This drawing explores the transparency of the diaphanous curtains.

Right:
Through the shop window
The space is a tranquil sanctuary amid the mayhem of mid-town Manhattan.

Right:
The shop display
The products are semi-obscured by the translucent curtain.

Far right:
Shop interior
Light is filtered through the curtains.

Interior control: Focus study 5

Name:
Qiora store and spa

Location:
New York, USA

Date:
2001

Designer:
Architecture Research Office (ARO)

Although fabric in the interior has a temporary and ephemeral character, it can control movement and delineate space in a subtle and sensitive manner.

Qiora, which means 'the light within', is the name of the holistic skincare brand launched by Japan's Shiseido Cosmetics in 2001. ARO were commissioned to design this New York flagship store, which combines an upmarket shop with a daytime 'spa'. The store, which is positioned on Madison Avenue, a busy Manhattan thoroughfare, needed to project the soothing qualities of the cosmetics. It had to exude calmness and inner serenity amid the chaos of the busy mid-town location.

The designers have used light and texture to create the calming atmosphere necessary to communicate the brand. From the outside, the tall, double-height space is visible through the large plate glass façade. The commercial shop is in the front of the space and the spa occupies the more discreet area at the rear. The spa itself consists of a series of cabins or free-standing cylinders where customers disrobe and are treated, and these are placed deep within the space. The use of curtains within an interior space is usually reserved for the decoration of domestic spaces, but within this store, ARO use a series of long organza veils to blur the boundaries between the spa and the retail space. The veils are full height, from ceiling to floor, and in order to screen off the more private spaces, the density of the fabric increases as it moves towards the rear of the space.

Artificial lights mounted on the perimeter walls create a bright atmospheric space that fluctuates in intensity between warmer and cooler, depending on the time of the day and the weather conditions outside the store. During the day white light illuminates the space while bluer tones are used in the evening to bring out the colour and texture of the space and the veils. At night, from the outside, the store has the appearance of a glowing lantern.

In this way, the designers have used two simple materials – artificial light and fabric – to create an interior of great control, atmosphere and character.

Many of the methods of organising and assembling interior space have been presented and a number of specialist terms introduced. These have been collected together in the following glossary to provide an easy reference section. Whilst it is impossible to be exhaustive, a good number of the terms that are the common language and terminology of interior design and architecture today are shown.

Acoustics The scientific study of sound and sound waves. The particular acoustic properties of an interior can be manipulated through the use of sound absorbent materials and fractured surfaces, both of which affect the reverberation time and reduce distortion and echo.

Adaptation The process of transforming an existing building to accommodate new uses. This is also referred to as remodelling, adaptive reuse and interior architecture.

Analysis The act of exploring and studying an existing building. This can be done in a variety of ways in order to extract the meaningful qualities of the building. These can prompt or stimulate the process of transforming the space.

Aperture An opening, such as a window or door, within the fabric of a building that allows view, light and air in and out of an interior.

Applied texture Added material such as metal, fabric, plastic or timber that can be applied to an existing surface in order to create or shape the new visual and atmospheric identity of an interior.

Arcade An enclosed passage or walkway covered with a series of arches or vaults supported on columns or piers. Shopping arcades usually have a central passageway with retail units on either side.

Aspect Aspect indicates the particular direction in which the viewer or building is facing.

Atrium Originally an uncovered Roman courtyard, the term is now commonly used to describe a covered interior space that usually has a glazed roof which allows sunlight and warmth to enter an interior.

Axis An imaginary line that usually runs through the centre of a space or building, it is used as a planning device and is related to symmetry. Axial planning can be used to arrange an interior in straight lines or in a way that prioritises certain qualities such as a view through the space or emphasises hierarchy.

Beam The beam is a core component of a basic structural frame. It is a horizontal bar, usually made from masonry, steel, or timber that is supported on either end.

Bioclimatic design The process of incorporating environmental issues into the practice of design.

Black water Sewage; it cannot be reused.

Building Regulations The design and construction of buildings and interiors are all subject to specific regulations that control issues such as planning, access and health and safety within the building. Specific regulations also govern the process of consent and permission to construct buildings.

Canopy A covering erected to provide protection from the elements or to emphasise a particular activity. A canopy is often found at the entrance to a building, but it can also be free-standing.

Circulation Circulation denotes the methods of movement within a building. Circulation is often arranged as a series of routes horizontally through a building via walkways, corridors and bridges, or vertically via stairs, ramps, lifts and escalators.

Cladding Cladding is often described as the application of a layer of material that will cover the structure of a building or element. On the outside of a building this may have to consider weathering and climate control. In an interior, cladding is more important in terms of performance, look and identity. The relationship between cladding and structure and its visual appearance is a complex issue that dominates architectural and design history. See Loos 'Ornament and Crime' 1908.

Classical Classical architecture derives its principles from Greek and Roman art and architecture. The main orders of classical architecture are Tuscan, Doric, Ionic, Corinthian and Composite. In its revived style it is known as neo-classicalism.

Clerestory The upper stage of the main walls of a church, often with windows or openings to admit light into the building.

Colonnade A device for controlling movement and space, it consists of a series of regularly placed columns that support a roof.

Column The column along with the beam forms the basic component of the structural system. It is the vertical element of the frame and is usually made from masonry, steel or timber.

Composition Composition is the plan or arrangement of elements in a visual design. In interior planning it relates to the organisation of the components of space. In elevation or section composition can relate to the deployment of rooms and interior elements in the building.

Conservation Conservation is the art of conserving existing structures in their present form or returning them back to their original state.

Context In Interior Architecture the context consists of the conditions surrounding the building to be reused. These conditions may be in close proximity or far away and have a variety of impacts upon the new interior.

Courtyard A space between or behind a building which is usually open to the elements and is enclosed by walls.

Climate The long-term or prevalent weather conditions of an area. The study of climatic conditions can be used to develop elements that control the atmosphere within the interior space.

Detail The finalising of a space and the application of materials and surfaces to an interior scheme is known as detailing. This often involves joinery, the application of materials and sometimes prototyping through mock-ups and samples.

DPC The damp-proof course is a barrier that is designed to prevent moisture rising through the walls of a structure. It is usually a plastic layer incorporated at low level into the walls of a building during construction, or can be retrospectively fitted by pumping silicone into holes drilled into the wall.

Element Within an interior, a specific object such as a piece of furniture or a room is described as an element within the space.

Elevation An elevation is a drawing usually of an outside wall or façade of a building. It is a two-dimensional representation of a wall showing the position of windows, doors and any other details of the building exterior.

Engineer The structural, civil, mechanical, electrical, environmental, acoustic and lighting engineers are often consulted by architects and designers in the design of buildings and their interiors.

Environment The context of a building and its interior, as well as the climatic issues that effect the design scheme or existing building.

Ephemeral Short-lived or transitory. Interiors are often described as ephemeral because of their temporary quality.

Ergonomics The study of spatial relationships and proportions in relation to the human body. This is exemplified by the *New Metric Handbook*, a book that catalogues these relationships and sets out the 'standards' of ergonomic reasoning.

ETFE foil Ethyl tetra fluoro ethylene foil is a strong, transparent and lightweight plastic. A piece of ETFE weighs less than one percent of a piece of glass with the same volume, it is a better insulator than glass, and it is much more resistant to solar gain.

Façade Quite simply the façade is the exterior front plane of a building.

Found object An object that has been removed from its natural situation and placed in an unusual context or situation.

Found texture When working with existing buildings found surfaces within the space can be retained and used to provide a meaningful connection to the history of the site.

Function The use of a space, either new or old, will often be referred to as the function of the space. Quite often function will also be referred to as 'the programme' of the interior or the accommodation brief for the new design.

Furniture/furnishings The character of a particular room can be created by the furniture, which can either be custom-made or selected by the designer.

Genius loci The particular and distinct 'spirit' of a place or building.

Gesamtkunstwerk The 'total work of art' or the notion that the designer is responsible for not only the space but also the all the details, even to the smallest such as a door handle. It has been known for the designer to take this to the extreme of creating the clothing to be worn within the space.

Grey water The waste water generated from domestic processes such as bathing, dishwashing and laundry. Grey water is often reused, especially in the garden.

Hierarchy When organising and planning space, the term hierarchy is sometimes used to distinguish primary and secondary elements within a design. It may also be used to classify major and minor functions within a space.

HVAC Acronym for heating ventilation and air conditioning.

Interior architecture Interior architecture is the practice of remodelling existing buildings. As well as the robust reworking of a building, interior architecture often deals with complex structural, environmental and servicing problems. It is sometimes referred to as adaptation, adaptive reuse or remodelling.

Interior decoration Interior decoration is the art of decorating inside spaces and rooms to impart a particular character and atmosphere to the room. It is often concerned with such issues as surface pattern, ornament, furniture, soft furnishings and lighting.

Interior design Interior design is an interdisciplinary practice that is concerned with the creation of a range of interior environments that articulate identity and atmosphere, through the manipulation of spatial volume, the placement of specific objects and furniture and the treatment of surfaces.

Intervention Intervention is a procedure that activates the potential or repressed meaning of a specific place. It truly works when the architectural response of the modifications draw all of their cues from the existing building.

Insertion The placement of a complete object within the confines of an existing building. It is a practice that establishes an intense relationship between the original building and the inserted element and yet allows the character of each to exist in a strong and independent manner.

Installation Installation is the strategy of placing a series or group of related elements within the context of an existing building. This is a process that will heighten the awareness of an existing building without adversely affecting it.

Insulation A material that is usually placed between the inner and outer layers of a wall to help maintain the constant temperature of an interior. Insulation can also be used to stop noise transfer from one room to another.

Light The manipulation of both natural and artificial light is an important consideration when designing interior space.

Light-shelf A device usually hung within a window to reflect natural light deep into an interior space.

Listed building When a building, an interior or even a monument or bridge is considered to be of historic importance or of cultural significance and therefore in need of protection from demolition or any insensitive changes, it is placed upon a protected building list. The listing usually takes the form of a grading of importance from one through to three. Both the exterior and interior of a building may be listed.

Load bearing Load bearing refers to the structural system employed to construct buildings. Buildings are usually constructed from masonry and are built up brick by brick from the ground.

Louvre Thin horizontal planes that are usually fashioned from timber or steel, and are placed on the outside of an opening to protect the interior from direct sunlight.

Materials The actual substances that are used to shape and order an interior. Commonly used materials are wood, glass, steel, plastic and stone, as well as textiles.

Microclimate The immediate environmental conditions of a particular site, building or space.

Mixed-use A building or interior that contains more than one function; for example, a development may combine retail with housing.

Monocoque A construction technique that uses the external skin of the object for structural support. The internal structure and the skin are unified as a single element. This is a method of construction most prevalent in aircraft and automotive design, but is beginning to be used as an architectural technique.

Narrative Narrative is a story or a text that describes a sequence of characters and events. In architecture and design, narrative is used to describe the stories or the sequence of events that the designer may wish to convey: the existing building, the exhibition design, the concept or the brand or identity.

Natural ventilation The process of supplying air to an interior by natural means, rather than using air conditioning. Natural ventilation makes use of windows, doors, grills and rooflights.

Object A purposefully placed object is loaded with meaning; whether it is a small piece of furniture, a large sculpture or a number of pieces clustered together, it establishes a physical and cultural relationship with its environment.

Occupation The use or inhabitation of an interior.

Opaque Not transmitting any light.

Orangery A classical greenhouse or conservatory traditionally used to grow oranges.

Organisation Organisation can be described as the planning or arrangement of a space; that is the objects, rooms and elements.

Ornament Ornament is a decorative detail than can be used to embellish parts of a building or an interior. It is often superfluous and it became a highly debated element of design in the twentieth century.

Orientation The direction in which a space is facing, used especially when a relationship is established between the interior and another object or feature.

Orthogonal The use of right angles within a design.

Overhang A projection from the edge of a building such as a roof or a balcony.

Patination Derived from the word patina, patination describes the change in the surface texture or pattern over time.

Pediment A classical element that is in the form of a low pitched gable and is usually found above a portico, although it can often be found above windows and doors.

Plane The façade, wall, ceiling and floor are regarded as the essential 'planes' of the interior of a building.

Planning The organisation of an interior by arranging the rooms, spaces and structure in a two-dimensional drawing.

Plaster A smooth covering for interior surfaces. It is applied when wet and can be smoothed over existing substrates to hide any imperfections or cracks.

Portal A structural frame that allows large spans to be covered without the use of excess amounts of columns, often used in the construction of large shed buildings. Portal is a term that can also be used to describe a porch or portico.

Portico A roofed space, often open or partly enclosed, that forms the entrance to a building. It developed in early Greek architecture, and is often supported by columns and can be a grand device on the façade of a building.

Promenade One of Le Corbusier's five points of architecture, it is the modernist concept of continual movement through a building. This journey is also referred to as architectural promenade.

PVB A plastic layer that is sandwiched between two sheets of glass in order to control solar gain and diffuse daylight.

Ramp An inclined plane that is used to connect differing levels within a building or an exterior space. It can be straight or curved and sometimes is used to make a dramatic statement within an interior. Various access laws such as DDA (Disability Discrimination Act) govern the angle of the incline.

Readymade The development of art from utilitarian everyday found objects not normally considered as art in their own right. The term Readymade was coined by the artist Marcel Duchamp, who created a series of objets d'art from such items as a bicycle wheel, a bottle rack and a urinal.

Recycling The process of reusing materials and buildings to create something new.

Reflection pool A strategically positioned, usually shallow, pool of water that reflects light into or around a building.

Render The application of a smooth plaster finish to an exterior wall.

Renovation Renovation is the process of renewing and updating a building. The function will remain the same and the structure is generally untouched, but the manner in which the building is used will be brought up to date. It is usually the services that require attention, especially the heating and sanitary systems.

Remodelling Remodelling is the process of wholeheartedly altering a building. The function is the most obvious change, but other alterations may be made to the building such as its structure, circulation routes and its orientation. Additions may be constructed whilst other areas may be demolished.

Restoration Restoration is the process of returning the condition of the building to its original state and this often involves using materials and techniques of the original period to ensure that the building appears as though it has just been constructed.

Reuse The transformation of an existing building may also be described as 'reuse'; a term that suggests that the elements and parts of both new and old buildings are reworked in order to create a new space. See also Adaptation, Remodelling and Interior architecture.

Section At any point on the plan of a building, the designer may describe a line through the drawing and visualise a vertical cut through the spaces. This is called a section. It will explain the volumes of the spaces and indicate the position of the walls, the floors, the roof and other structural elements.

Sequence Sequence is a term used to describe the order of interior spaces that the designer intends the visitor to experience in their journey through the space.

Site-specific The site is the specific location or context of a building or space. Site-specific is a phrase used to describe the influences that are derived directly from the particular conditions found on site.

Solar gain The increase in temperature that derives from the warmth of the sun as it enters a space or falls upon an object.

Spolia Spolia describes the act of reusing building elements and applying them to new or later monuments. It derives from the phrase 'the spoils of war' where the victors in battle would take trophies from their foes.

Stack effect The process of warm air rising though a space or building and being replaced with cooler air at low level. This natural process can be used to cool a space or building.

Structure A structure denotes a shelter, or an enclosure that distinguishes inside and outside space. Structure is one of the basic elements of the construction of space and usually takes the form of materials assembled in such a way as to withstand the pressures put upon them.

Stucco A smooth or decorated plaster finish to a wall. Decorative stucco reached its zenith in the florid architectural styles of the Baroque and Rococo.

Sustainability In architecture and design, sustainability refers to the sensible use of natural resources and materials that does not deplete them in an unnecessary or wasteful way. It also refers to the sourcing and use of methods of construction and certain materials that do not contribute to climate change through the exhaustion of natural resources or their transport across the world.

Threshold The threshold is the point of transition between two spaces, whether this is inside and outside or two interior spaces.

Translucent Permitting light to pass through a material, while still obscuring the view. Coloured or stained glass, acrylic, alabaster and thin sheets of marble all have this property.

Transparent Allowing the transmission of light and view through a material. Clear, untextured glass is the most obvious example of this type of material.

Truss A truss is a number of beams and/or rafters tied together to form a bridging element.

Urbanism The study of cities, their evolution and development.

View The view is usually the image of a scene, typically a pleasant picture through an opening or from the building.

Weather boarding Weather boarding is a cladding method that uses timber to cover a building by successively overlapping each member; this allows the rain to run off and make a watertight seal.

Weathering The change in the surface of a building, interior or specific material due to prolonged exposure to the environment.

Graeme Brooker would like to thank Howard Cooper and Shelley McNulty (Interior Design team at Manchester Metropolitan University) for their relentless support and Claire Brooker for her dedicated patience.

Sally Stone would like to thank Pilar Cos for her time and inspiration, Tomeu Ferra for his generosity and hospitality, Gillian Ward for her forebearance, Reuben, Ivan and Agnes for their buoyancy and Dominic Roberts for his sustained resilience.

Both Graeme Brooker and Sally Stone would like to thank Aaron Losada for his excellent drawings; Michael Coates for his useful assistance; MIRIAD (Manchester Institute of Research in Art and Design) for their financial assistance; and all of the designers and photographers who have lent their work for publication. Finally, thanks to AVA Publishing, especially Leafy Robinson, for their persistent encouragement throughout the project.

Images

All diagrams by Aaron Losada and images © Graeme Brooker and Sally Stone, except for:
003: photograph courtesy of Ben Kelly Design
016: photograph © Iuri
018: photographs by Hélène Binet (top), and David Stewart (bottom);
019: photograph by David Stewart; diagrams by 5th Studio
021: photograph © 0399778584
026+027: photographs and diagrams courtesy of Architects Britch
030+031: photographs and diagrams courtesy of Stephenson Bell Architects
032: photographs courtesy of Bill Dunster Architects
037: photograph courtesy of Ben Kelly Design
038+039: photographs and diagrams courtesy of Ben Kelly Design
041: photographs © Roland Halbe/artur
043: photograph © Lluís Casals
049: photograph (bottom) © Sarah Blee; diagrams courtesy of Neutelings Riedijk Architects
050+051: photographs courtesy of Ben Kelly Design
054+055: photographs © Paul Ott
065: photograph © Patricia Hofmeester
066: photograph © Salamanderman
068+069: photographs by Dominic Roberts

072: photograph courtesy of ONL
074: photograph (bottom) © Philip Lange; photograph (top) © Rafael Ramirez Lee
075: photograph © Rafael Ramirez Lee
076: photographs © Mark Bond
077: photograph © David Quixley
080+081: photographs by Dominic Roberts
083: photograph by Hélène Binet
084+085: photographs and diagrams courtesy of Richard Murphy Architects
088+089: photographs by Dominic Roberts; diagram courtesy O'Donnell + Tuomey
090: photograph by Paul Smoothy
093: image by KDa
094+095: photographs by Dominic Roberts
096+097: photographs by Dominic Roberts
100+101: photographs and drawing courtesy of Arca
102: drawing courtesy of Diller Scofidio + Renfro
103: photograph (bottom) courtesy of Diller Scofidio + Renfro
106: photographs courtesy of Latz + Partner
107: photograph (left) by Michael Latz
108+109: Images and drawings courtesy of KDa
110: photograph by Eamon Canniffe
114+115: photographs by Peter Cook, courtesy of View Pictures Ltd; diagrams courtesy of Wright & Wright Architects

116+117: photographs by Paul Smoothy; drawing courtesy of LTS Architects
122+123: photograph (top) © Bruno Medley; photograph (bottom) © Steve Baker; drawing courtesy of Foster + Partners
124: drawings courtesy of Neutelings Riedijk Architects
127: photographs and drawings courtesy of Francis Roberts Architects
130+131: photographs by Dominic Roberts
132: photographs by John Lee
139: photographs by Peter Aaron/Esto, courtesy of View Pictures Ltd
140: photographs by Piemonti Giovanna, courtesy of Massimiliano Fuksas
143: photograph (middle) © Stephen Finn
144+145: photographs © Keith Hunter
149: photograph courtesy of ARO
150+151: photograph courtesy Joe Jessop
152+153: photographs by Dominic Roberts
154+155: photographs by Dominic Roberts
158: photographs courtesy of Bernard Tschumi Architects
160: photographs courtesy of Ben Kelly Design
162: photographs courtesy of Jonathan Adams
164: diagram courtesy of LOT-EK
168+169: photographs courtesy of ARO

Pull quotes

015: Los, S. 1995. *Carlo Scarpa – An Architectural Guide*. Verona: Arsenale Editrice srl
017: Giancarlo De Carlo, quoted in McKean, J. 2004. *Giancarlo De Carlo – Layered Places*. Fellbach: Edition Axel Menges
021: Holl, S. 1996. *Anchoring*. New York, NY: Princeton Architectural Press
023: Cullen, G. 1996. *The Concise Townscape*. Oxford: The Architectural Press
024: Sanin, F. 1994. *Münster City Library – Architecture In Detail*. London: Phaidon
031: Breitling, S. Cramer, J. 2007. *Architecture in Existing Fabric – Planning Design Building*. Basel: Birkhäuser
040: Brooker, G. & Stone, S. 2004. *Rereadings*. London: RIBA
043: Silvetti, J. 1997. Interactive realms: The bridge of San Francesco and the Palazzo Sant'Elia. In: A. Von Hoffman, (ed). *Form, Modernism and History, Essays in Honor of Eduard F. Sekler*, Harvard: University Press.
045: Adam Caruso, quoted in Pearman, H. 2005. Caruso St. John celebrate their trad influences. *Architects' Journal*, 6 October.
047: Citation from the Pritzker Jury, Pritzker Architecture Prize Laureate 1985, taken from *The Pritzker Architecture Prize* website. 2008 [online]. [Accessed 3rd January 2008]. Available from the World Wide Web: www.pritzkerprize.com/full_new_site/hollein_citation.htm
048: Alexander, C. 1977. *A Pattern Language*. Oxford: Oxford University Press
057: Lynch, K. 1960. *The Image of the City*. Cambridge, MA: MIT Press
067: Powell, K. 1999. *Architecture Reborn*. London: Laurence King Publishing
068: Lazarus, M.A., Mandler, S. Odell, W. 2006. *The Guidebook to Sustainable Design*. Chichester: John Wiley & Sons

071: Zumthor, P. 1998 Architecture and Urbanism Extra. February
075: Rapoport, A. 1969. *House Form and Culture*. New Jersey: Prentice Hall
079: Roberts, D. 2006. Interventions. Artimide
085: Cullen, G. 1971. *The Concise Townscape*. Oxford: Architectural Press
095: Langhorne, J. 1774–47. The Country Justice
097: Caldenby, C., Lindvall, J., Wang, W. (eds). 1998. *20th Century Architecture: Sweden*. New York: Prestel
101: Deplazes, A. (ed) 2005. *Constructing Architecture: Materials, Processes, Structures – A Handbook*. Basel: Birkhäuser
103: Dimendberg, E. 2003. Blurring Genres. In: Betsky, A. et al (eds). *Scanning: The Aberrant Architectures of Diller + Scofidio*. New York: Whitney Museum of American Art
104: Tagliabue, B. 2004. EMBT: *Work in Progress*. New York: Actar D
107: Boyer, M.C. 1996. *The City of Collective Memory*. Cambridge, MA: The MIT Press
111: Brooker, G. and Stone, S. 2007. *Gli Interni Nel Progetto Sull'esistente: Tradizione E Ricerca*. Padova: Il Poligrafo
112: Wright, J. of Shed 54. 2000 In conversation with the authors, 20th October 2000.
115: Edwards, B. and Hyett, P. 2001. *Rough Guide to Sustainability*. London: RIBA Publishing
116: Allen, G. Lyndon, D. Moore, C. 1974. *The Place of Houses*. New York: Henry Holt Publishers
125: McLennan, J. F. 2004. *The Philosophy of Sustainable Design*. Bainbridge Island, WA: Ecotone
129: Pallasmaa, J. 2005. *Encounters*. Helsinki: Rakennustieto Publishing

131: Caldenby, C., Lindvall, J., Wang, W. (eds). 1998. *20th Century Architecture: Sweden*. New York: Prestel
137: Edwards, B. and Hyett, P. 2001. *Rough Guide to Sustainability*. London: RIBA Publishing
139: Kalkin, A. 2002. *Architecture and Hygiene*. London: B.T. Batsford
141: Scott, F. 2007. *On Altering Architecture*. London: Routledge
145: Lazarus, M.A., Mandler, S. Odell, W. 2006. *The Guidebook to Sustainable Design*. Chichester: John Wiley & Sons
151: Weston, R. 2004. *Plans Sections Elevations: Key Buildings of the Twentieth Century*. London: Laurence King Publishing
152: The Energy Research Group (Owen Lewis, J. (ed)). 1999. A Green Vitruvius: Principles and Practice of Sustainable Architectural Design. London: James & James (Science Publishers)
156: Houben, F./Mecanoo Architects. 2001. *Composition Contrast Complexity*. Basel: Birkhäuser
159: Tschumi, B. 1990. *Questions of Space*. Architectural Association Publishers
163: Leitner, B. 1994. 'Le Cylindre Sonore'. In: Martin, E. (ed). 1994. *Architecture as a translation of music* (Pamphlet Architecture 16). New Jersey: Princeton Architectural Press
167: Partington, R. in an interview with *Laminated Glass News* [online]. [Accessed 15th January 2008] www.dupont.com/safetyglass/lgn/stories/1105.html
168: Sanders, J. 2002. 'Curtain Wars: Architects, Decorators and the Twentieth-Century Domestic Interior'. In *Harvard Design Magazine*, No.16, pp.14–20

Context + Environment